W9-BSZ-619

HOW TO HANDLE YOUR OWN PUBLIC RELATIONS

HOW TO HANDLE YOUR OWN PUBLIC RELATIONS

H. GORDON LEWIS

EMERSON COLLEGE LIBRARY

Nelson-Hall
Chicago

HM
263
L474
1976

Copyright © 1976 by H. Gordon Lewis
Second Printing, 1977

All rights reserved. No part of this book may be reproduced
in any form without permission in writing from the publisher,
except by a reviewer who wishes to quote brief passages in
connection with a review written for broadcast or for inclusion
in a magazine or newspaper. For information address Nelson-Hall
Inc., Publishers, 325 W. Jackson Blvd., Chicago, Illinois 60606.

Manufactured in the United States of America.

Library of Congress Cataloging in Publication Data

Lewis, Herschell Gordon, 1926–
    How to handle your own public relations.

    Includes index.
    1. Public relations. 2. Publicity. I. Title.
HM263.L474   659.2   76–20710
ISBN 0—88229-319-2 (cloth)
ISBN 0—88229-408-2 (paper)

contents

*Apartment Buildings ● Audio-Visual Dealerships ●
Automobile Dealerships ● Auto Parts Companies,
Rentals, Ancillaries ● Bakeries ● Banks ● Beauty
Salons ● Beverage Distributorships ● Book
Stores ● Bridal Shops ● Bus Lines ● Camps ●
Carpet Cleaners ● Catering Businesses ● Clothing
Stores ● Contracting/Developing Operations ●
Department Stores ● Dog Kennels ● Employment
Agencies ● Finance Companies ● Florist Shops ●*

preface

Every textbook or manual I've ever read treats public relations as though it were brain surgery.

The reverence for form, for background, for being able to do one thing before one dares try another—these suggest a difficulty that simply doesn't exist in today's marketplace.

There's no question that the professional public relations man can, through his specialized background, his contacts, and his dedication of time, accomplish more than a business-person or someone in an organization who carries the title "Director of Public Relations"—meaning that he or she has the unhappy task of trying to get that organization's name in the paper.

But there's also no question that the amateur can succeed in public relations. Today. Without serving an apprenticeship or learning a bunch of mystic incantations.

What this book suggests is that you not succumb to the propaganda suggesting that one needs twenty-seven years of hard experience and the first name of every newsman in town in order to compete. You can prove this claim two hours from now—by reading on.

acknowledgments

It was Charlotte Bell, who answers my phone, who said to me, "When are you going to write that book on public relations?"

It was Pamela Orsinger, who types (and corrects) almost every word I write, who kept the project going, since I had to stay at least two manuscript pages ahead of her.

It was Margo Nelson, who sits at my right arm, who agreed to organize the index after spending months organizing me.

And it was my wife, Helene, whose own professional career has been 100 percent in public relations, who pointed out mistakes and logical gaps, professionally instead of personally.

That I am in debt to four charming women bothers me not at all. It's one reason why a book that ten years ago might have referred to "public relations man" now refers, with complete accuracy, to "public relations person."

Ladies—I thank you.

1   oh, yes, you can!

Since public relations is not only an inexact profession, but in the minds of some critics a nonprofession, any book on the subject which explodes the myth that public relations, like brain surgery, should be practiced only by tested and licensed specialists must attract some criticism.

Yes, I'm hopeful that one day public relations will reach a high point of professionalism. I'm hopeful that, within the lifetime of my great-grandchildren, in order to be a public relations specialist an individual will have to prove that he knows what he is doing; that he will have demonstrable abilities in mass communications and group psychology; that he will have at least competitive literacy; and that he will take, in all seriousness, an oath of professional ethics.

Public relations is not even within sight of these goals; the "profession" itself is fragmented, and the standards of professional organizations, membership in which is largely social,

1

are uneven. For simple proof, call three or four public relations companies and ask for presentations. How many of them
will offer you *specifics* rather than a Knute Rockne half-time
pep talk? How many of them can talk about marketing benefits rather than press exposure? How many will have any
really original ideas?

(It should be noted that public relations companies quite
logically dislike speculative presentations for which they receive no money. Request for a list of suggested projects will
serve just as well. A lunch at which you ask for specific ideas
will prove creative imagination or lack of it.)

Fortunately for you (and me), practicing public relations intelligently isn't as difficult as rebuilding the carburetor
of your car. This is because the mechanical aspects of public
relations are fairly well known to most people who watch the
news on television, listen to it on the radio, and read it in the
newspaper. All they have missed is relating it to themselves.
How might *their* names appear? How might *they* write or
be the subject of a feature story in a trade publication?

It is my hope that reading and thinking about the pertinent pages of this guide will give you some answers. Whether
you put any of them into practice depends on your own state
of mind. As you well know, fear of embarrassment, of seeming "pushy," of making a promotional mistake, of starting
something that will backfire or not come off, are reasons so
many fail to capitalize on obvious promotional opportunities.

If I may make a single suggestion to generate the proper
attitude while reading this book, let it be this:

Since benefits seldom come to those who fail to seek
them out, seek them out; since no one else will start the promotional machinery working for you, you start it; since so
many worthwhile image-builders and attention-getters depend
on nothing other than intelligent application of time and effort, apply time and effort intelligently; and since the only
missing component may well be technique, not intent, borrow

the techniques. Whatever happens, you'll be way ahead of the person who has done nothing at all.

Rules of the Game

Two rules should govern the entrepreneur's handling of public relations activities:

1. Always act as though you know what you're doing. In public relations, confidence (or the appearance of it) often is a valid replacement for knowledge, especially when dealing with media people.

2. When self-puffery seems too apparent, appoint an employee to be "director of public relations" and have him or her front the activity. Removed from the firing line, you're in a more dispassionate position and have a better opportunity to create a "willing suspension of disbelief." All may know that you're guiding the project, but you haven't been obvious about it.

Etch Rule One in stone. Reporters, columnists, and television crews hover like vultures around a promotion they feel has been approached with less than total confidence. They tend to equate confidence with professionalism, and your knowledge of this fact is a primary weapon in the promotional wars.

Several other rules *must* be followed as you, the pretender, invade the domain of the public relations princes. The rules are neither spectacularly difficult nor arcane; in fact, they are all reasonable and sensible. Here they are, for the dilettante who would masquerade successfully as a journeyman:

1. Your grammar, spelling, and punctuation must be impeccable. There really isn't any excuse for misspelled words or two sentences linked by a comma, especially since everyone has access to someone whose own vanity is flattered when he or she is asked to proofread something.

2. News releases should follow the professional form outlined in Chapter 3.

3. Never begin a project you can't complete. If you announce a contest and no one enters, you still must preserve the facade to the end.

4. If you know your results will be amateurish, don't do it. Unedited home movie film is too easily compared with professional footage.

5. Every week, meet or at least talk with one editor, reporter, or personality. It's refreshing for them, too, to talk occasionally with someone who isn't asking for an immediate favor. And within six months you'll have the most solid contact list on your block.

6. Resist the temptation to show off how much you know.

7. When you make a speech or an appearance, remember that the word *a* is usually pronounced "uh" and that contractions (he's, they'll, won't, can't, wouldn't) help take the stiltedness off a speech.

8. Occasionally make an effort to boost someone other than yourself. *That's* public relations.

9. Every morning, as you shave or pluck your eyebrows (or both), look into the mirror and tell yourself what you're going to do that day to build image or increase public awareness.

10. Never try a foolish stunt that results in your being regarded as a clown. Dignity is implicit in professionalism.

These may not be as profound as the original ten commandments; but in the volatile, dynamic world of public relations, they're certainly more practical than ten "thou shalt nots."

Do It Yourself

The mystery of public relations is largely self-imposed. In-groups wallow in terminology rather than knowledge. And the fact that a book like this could be published is itself an indication of the uncertainty, let alone the chicanery, that besets what one day will be a profession reserved for the "pros" but isn't yet.

One of the great areas of confusion is the use of the word *publicity* as a synonym for *public relations*. Especially in large cities, where newspaper columns and television interview shows often are run by and for in-groups, some professionals in public relations exist only because they have contacts, not because they have marketing knowledge. "I'll get your name in the paper, baby" becomes a logical reason to hire a public relations person; thus, client as well as practitioner becomes a convert to a byproduct of true public relations.

Almost all of what these people do, however, can be done by a business owner, organization chairman, or club president himself or herself. And much of what even a knowledgeable, thoughtful professional public relations organization does also can be handled with equivalent professionalism by a businessman whose ego isn't on the line and who isn't afraid of the term-throwers and obfuscators who seem to abound in these waters.

This is a "how to" book. The theory of mass communications evolves constantly, and this book is designed specifically as a manual, a handbook, a reference. Thus, no apology is extended for some of the hard-boiled and even cynical suggestions crammed into these pages. If any apology is in order, it might be to the public relations professionals whose integrity gives hope to the profession and who might object to what they believe is an oversimplification of complex communications methods.

Why might a business or professional person decide to dip a toe into the boiling rapids of public relations? The primary reason is that competition demands it; if the theatre across the street is air-conditioned, you'd better start getting estimates. But another reason is that it makes no sense to bypass a logical and worthwhile means of building image, drawing attention, and achieving recognition without having to pay advertising dollars.

Since the typical public relations practitioner lives in the half-world of competition, fear, and misunderstanding, he has a problem other than the announced problem of image-building for his client; he has the problem of *pleasing* that client, delivering what that client wants.

Years ago, I used to feel that there was a huge gap between "us"—the educated public relations professionals—and "them"—the white-on-white-shirted, suede-shoed, name-dropping publicity men. Like most PR men and women who would try to get clients by promising undreamed-of benefits from a long-range image-building campaign, I would make written presentations in vinyl binders with the would-be client's name stamped in gold. In those presentations, I'd suggest projects that I knew would justify the six-month-minimum retainer contract I'd brought along.

As the art of public relations evolves (often in a line oblique to Darwinian evolution), I no longer feel strongly about the "publicity" versus "public relations" differential. Perhaps this is because the competitive clamor for publicity has meant that clients demand more of it; perhaps it is because we've learned a little about how to combine image-building with name-dropping; or perhaps it's because publicity has become more difficult to deliver when a typical columnist's office is bombarded with hundreds of non-newsworthy name-dropping items every day. Furthermore, some of the image-building methods have become easier to deliver as more business and professional people become willing to experiment in this area.

There never has been any question about the ability of a business owner or an organization chairman, for example, to compete in public relations. The question always has been one of execution. Afraid to make an ass of himself, the businessman will pay a thousand dollars to a PR person to set up a news conference. What does the professional do that the businessman might not do for himself? He makes five major contributions:

1. He begins with a base of contacts developed over the years. These contacts assure some attendance at the event.

2. He stages the news conference in a professional manner, so that media representatives will know that this isn't run by a bunch of beginners.

3. He prepares a press kit with news releases and fact sheets, which he hands out to the newsmen who attend.

4. He socializes and smooths so that the net effect will be positive; and he takes the sponsoring individual off the firing line—an inevitable problem if one man does it all.

5. He acts as instructor, showing those staging the news conference how to handle their own presentations and how to avoid amateurism.

Except for having a base of contacts, there is nothing here the individual could not do for himself. And contacts themselves are always "iffy" in a revolving-door profession.

I'm not suggesting that someone whose business is manufacturing buttonhole-making machinery is, per se, as powerful a public relations man as is someone who does PR for a living, any more than I might suggest that a public relations person could survive in the competitive world of buttonhole-making machines. I'm not that naive. Rather, I am suggesting that the businessman who might never stage that news conference *at all* might be inspired to do it by using the techniques and suggestions described in this book. At least he'll know that he isn't developing a severe case of foot-in-mouth disease.

2 public relations, publicity, and your image

No one—not even the federal government—can anticipate that its news stories, its carefully staged public relations
activities, or its internally approved methodology will be welcomed by the audience at which it is aimed *unless* the material
used as weaponry to build image or to motivate the outsider
is of interest to that person.

Thus the challenge of public relations is not merely the
dissemination of information of interest to the disseminator;
it is, rather, the creation of materials that are apparently of
interest to the recipient, but that benefit the originator.

PR Is More Than Publicity

Modern public relations in no way is synonymous with
publicity. In these pages, you will see that comment made over
and over again. One reason for the emphasis is to spell out the
difference between the sophisticated public relations marketplace of the 1970s and 1980s and the relatively simple, artless
approach of the 1920s.

Some areas of information dissemination call for greater subtlety than others. "Show biz," for example, never has pretended that its news releases were anything other than blatant publicity. Whether Anna Held took a milk bath or Racquel Welch wore an oversized brassiere or Marlon Brando used cotton in his mouth for *The Godfather,* theatrical publicity in general is not and never has been intended as public relations. It represents, rather, a standing still—a throwback to a time when rock-'em, sock-'em publicity men gauged their success only by the number of lines of type a newspaper would give their clients.

This anachronism is still alive and well in the gossip columns carried by most metropolitan daily newspapers. If one were to analyze the information content of any such column, it would be clear immediately that here exists one of the last, fading outlets for the publicity man who does not have the tools, the weaponry, nor the attitude of his successor—the public relations man—any more than a Neanderthal man had the tools, the weapons, or the attitudes of modern man, who succeeded him but is historically in his debt.

News releases do remain the cornerstone of public relations. In that respect, the search for publicity remains "the right arm of the body." It might well be argued that in putting together an information package for the consumer (the consumer in this context being the person at whom publicity information is aimed and from whom a reaction is anticipated) the public relations function usurps the news function. One logically might ask: Isn't this part of the job that should be done by reporters?

But asking the question doesn't help the person who wants a favorable light cast on his own business, profession, or personal reputation. If media carried all the information that might be of even peripheral interest to its audience, not only would there not be such a profession as public relations, but the daily newspapers would be thousands of pages thick.

Access to the Media

Since so many interests clamor for favorable mention in news media, one does not have these outlets to himself. Those who succeed in getting media publicity ordinarily do so for one of three reasons:

1. That individual is a heavy advertiser who has "position" with that medium.

2. The lines of communication between that person and those responsible for the decision of what to print and what not to print are strong.

3. The information is indeed worthy of inclusion together with the day's news.

It should be obvious that a small business owner will not be able to compete with corporate giants on the first level and seldom on the second. But the public relations departments of American Telephone and Telegraph, U.S. Steel, General Motors, Ford Motor Company, Procter & Gamble, Sears, or any other "Fortune 500" company will tell you that despite the massive purchases of space and time by their companies in practically all media, only a fraction of the news releases they submit achieve circulation in those same media.

Thus, the argument that the individual or company who spends the most money has the best chance is only slightly true. In fact, at some news desks, the "Young Turks" prefer to reject information from these "malefactors of great wealth." There is validity to the idea that cultivation of a relationship with media will result in a higher percentage of releases being printed (occasionally in bylined feature stories). This is because the personal relationship enables one to request the favor of news coverage on a personal basis rather than a business one.

But there is a far more important reason for the success of this method. When you are on a first-name basis with, let us say, a news editor at a broadcast station or someone of authority at a local newspaper, you not only can request coverage; you also can ask that person for information that can help you increase the chances that your story will run. For example, you might well ask, prior to a special issue featuring automobiles (many newspapers have two such sections a year) what kind of story would be best suited for inclusion in that section. This gives you a powerful leg up over the competition, who won't have the benefit of this information. All things being equal, the news release you submit will be better received because it will better reflect the requirements of the publication in which it is to appear.

Obviously, too, an editor with a choice of stories to fill a limited amount of space is likely to select material submitted by someone with whom he has a personal relationship over the material of persons unknown to him. This is a normal personal reaction. But suppose that yours is the most professional, the most logical, the most informative of the stories that cross his desk that day. In such a case, personal relationships become less important. Whether you buy a lot of advertising space is less important too, although when the story runs, undoubtedly some major advertiser will say, "Why did you run a story about a company that spends so much less on advertising than I do?"

This whole question of the relationship between allocation of editorial space and how many ads are bought is a gray area. Many media deny emphatically that their editorial staffs are influenced at all by the advertising staff. With the exception of the large and powerful metropolitan newspapers and national magazines, such a claim is usually hogwash. It certainly is usually untrue in the case of community newspapers and broadcast stations. The advertising manager can and does demand that space be given to news releases submitted by heavy advertisers. In the case of some trade magazines, the advertiser who is being courted by the publication may strike a deal: "OK. I'll run a page if you'll run a feature on our company." Sometimes the publication, in a burst of statesmanship, will agree to run a story on the *industry*, featuring not only that advertiser but other companies as well. Ordinarily, though, the publication will say, "OK. Send us a story, and if it's usable we'll print it." In fact, the publication may offer to write the story based only on a fact sheet and photographs submitted by the company.

Suppose that yours is such a company and that a trade publication has agreed to run the story you submit. What should you say?

To submit a story that is nothing but puffery about your company would be to do a disservice not only to the reader-ship of that publication and to the publication itself but to your company as well. The readers aren't interested in you. That isn't why they subscribe to or read that publication. Obviously, if your story is so self-aggrandizing that it fails to recognize the interests of the readership, you will be the loser because your story won't be read.

Thus it behooves you to write a story of interest to the readership. In addition to the story's primary use on the pages of that publication, you should arrange wide secondary use of reprints of the article, distributed through the mail to prospective customers or clients. You needn't adopt a posture of self-effacement, but you should recognize the importance of the appearance of truth, the appearance of fact, the appearance of interest. This is the challenge we are talking about in the first place.

Image-Building

Why bother creating an image for your business? Why bother sending out news stories, demanding press coverage, distributing pamphlets and brochures and newsletters, and in general adding another area of work to what may be an already understaffed business?

The answer is that those businesses that tend to succeed

are those that have an *image*. If yours is a discount store, seek the image of *the* discount store. If yours is an automobile dealership, seek the image of the most aggressive or the most fastidious or the most exclusive or the highest-volume dealership in the area. If yours is a small manufacturing company, seek the image of the custom manufacturer or the company with the price advantage or the company with the instant inventory or, most difficult of all, the company manufacturing the finest quality. If yours is an insurance business, seek the image of extraordinary service or a never-sleep availability or the willingness to cover the unusual or perhaps even humorous risk.

Regardless of the type of business, decide logically and deliberately on the image you want and, following the rules laid down in these pages, build that image doggedly, repeatedly, consistently, and frequently—bearing in mind that although you yourself may become sick of the project and feel that it is overworked, the reader or listener or viewer occasionally exposed to those bits of information you send out will not feel that you have had too much coverage. He sees many other items too, and even if every word you write is printed and noted (which is not probable), it is just part of a continuing stream to the readership or audience.

Building an image is not accomplished by writing a bunch of adjectives about yourself. It is, rather, based on consistency of promotional approach. If, for example, you are determined to build an image for your insurance agency as the agency that insures *anything,* you should write a lighthearted news release whenever you have insured an unusual risk, even if that is only one minor coverage within the overall policy. You cannot wait for the circus to ask you to insure the lion's teeth or for a dancer to insure her legs. Rather, you select from what may be an ordinary policy those elements that are of interest because they insure a risk not normally known to the reader. This is the type of selective promotion that will build an image for you.

A word of warning: Don't ever embarrass a client or customer by exposing his name in your news stories without his permission. This can be a costly experiment. It's far easier to refer to the individual as "a client" or "a customer," unless he himself is the kind of person who welcomes news coverage. But don't take the risk. Always ask first.

Who Is Your Public?

Don't make the mistake of assuming that the only people you want to reach with your public relations campaign are those who are the most obvious prospective buyers of whatever it is you have to sell. There are other groups whose importance, while not as immediately apparent, is just as great:

1. Future buyers. This includes students, people who because of age or economic circumstances do not yet qualify as prime prospects, or people in other fields who might become customers.

2. Makers of opinion. This includes teachers, employers, purchasing agents, foremen, the press, or others who mold the opinion of the people you are trying to reach.

3. The competition. Odd as it may seem, the competition should be included in your information campaign. The image you present within the trade is just as important as the image you present to customers. If a competing company is looking for a merger, acquisition, or sellout, or perhaps for a cooperative venture, you might be a better candidate because of the image you have transmitted.

4. Businesses or industries of peripheral allied interests. If you manufacture greeting cards, the discount store area would be a logical target for you. If you sell photographic supplies, an industrial user might represent a single order that would far outweigh any ten individual orders you might have for that month.

5. Your own employees. Intramural public relations is almost as important as raises, because the owner or manager of the business has an opportunity to accomplish two im-

portant morale-lifting goals: recognition and ego-boosting for those who have accomplished something; and creation of a "family" atmosphere to reduce the arm's length approach which is too prevalent in labor/management relationships.

In short, your image should be transmitted to as wide a prospective group as possible. You are, after all, dealing with people. The average individual holds his job substantially less than five years and will not move vertically within a single company. The man who is assistant purchasing agent for ball bearings may two months from now be head purchasing agent for crane supplies, and you dare not miss him in your battle for image recognition.

"Just Spell My Name Right"

There was a time, during the 1920s *Front Page* approach to publicity, when a common instruction to a publicity man— usually theatrical—was "I don't care what you say. Just spell my name right."

Those days are gone forever. In fact, some celebrities in the nontheatrical world sometimes use their public relations people to try to keep their names *out* of the paper. This is not because of any sense of modesty, but because of pressures that could result on an economic level, because of ongoing negotiations with unions or other organizations, or because of some negative event that the individual does not want publicized. Examples might be divorce, negative financial news, legal actions, threatened or existing strikes, "secret" negotiations, or a story not yet ripe.

But the mere proper spelling of the name doesn't constitute public relations. In an image-conscious world, it isn't difficult for negative public relations to damage an image rather than enhance it, and a better philosophy for the late 1970s might be, "If you can't say something nice, don't say anything at all."

Incidentally, spelling the name right *is* important. Many

a news story has gone awry through the failure of someone to check the spelling, which has to be impeccable. In fact, often a public relations man will be blamed when a story appears in print with misspelled words and names. Even if it was a typesetter who butchered the spelling, the public relations person bears the brunt.

3 mechanical tools: the news release and photos

Let's go back to basics: In preparing material for publication, tell them what *they* want to read or hear, not what *you* want to read or hear.

The one key test of a news release is whether or not it reads like news. And the way to apply that test is to compare what you've written with other stories in the newspaper. Unfair, you say? You're comparing apples and oranges? Not true. Your story is a *news* release. Even though the editor may be your brother-in-law, at least give him an excuse to run the story. Unless it reads like news, you'd better be a heavy advertiser to anticipate the story's running at all.

Eliminating Adjectives

If there's one way to force a news release to read like news and not advertising, it's to go over it with a heavy pencil, mercilessly slashing out the adjectives. As an example:

> The most beautiful and magnificent Fords ever built by this famous manufacturer are being shown in the handsome showroom of Johnson Motors, one of the largest and best-known Ford dealers of this entire area.
>
> These wonderful motorcars have a new, exquisite velour upholstery. They are truly a triumph of engineering and design.

Forgetting the meaningless and noncommunicative cliché of "triumph of engineering and design" (a common error in casual writing about which more will be said), ask yourself: news or ad? An editor, reading this release, would know at once that not only would competitors howl with rage but his readers would learn nothing.

What are the objectionable words in this all-too-recognizable opening of a news release? The list is simply a list of the adjectives:

> *beautiful*
> *magnificent*
> *famous*
> *handsome*
> *best-known*
> *wonderful*
> *exquisite*

The reason for the exclusion of the word *new* from that list of noncommunicative words is that *new* has worth in news releases. Someone once said that *new* is three-fourths of *news;* the proportion isn't too high.

Without the puffery, the story might begin another way:

> "Dad, can I go sit in the car?"
>
> For nearly a century youngsters have asked that question; and finally Dad can nod and not worry about chewing gum or heel marks, according to a local auto dealer.
>
> The velour upholstery now standard in the new Fords, says Johnson Motors, maintains the feel and appearance of fine fabric but has a nonabsorptive finish that wipes clean with a damp cloth.

Putting Puffery in Quotes

Here's a sentence from a news story as submitted:

> Never have such bargains in furs been available. The public is invited to attend this extraordinary sale.

How can this sentence be saved, even including the cliché adjective *extraordinary*? Answer: By putting the thought into quotes. Doing this takes away the editorial pain of a seeming commercial endorsement, because the third-person comment has been replaced by a first-person comment:

> According to J. L. Johnson, president of Johnson Furs, "In my opinion this is the most extraordinary sale we've ever held."

Let's try it again:

> This is the highest honor any athlete at Norville High School has ever received. The entire community should be proud of him.

How much more readable and usable that sentence is when it is attributed to someone:

> "This is the highest honor any athlete at Norville High School has ever received," said Principal T. R. Woods. "The entire community should be proud of him."

Or try this sentence taken from a news release submitted by a civic club:

> The dynamic speaker thrilled his audience with his exciting photographs taken in the very heart of Peking.

If you would revise it something like this, you're thinking like a pro:

> Fred T. Graham, president of the club, called the speech "dynamic and thrilling." Said Graham, "The photographs themselves were especially exciting because they were taken in the very heart of Peking."

Graham said it, not the newspaper. The line between opinion and fact has been preserved, and the story is printable.

Simplifying Vocabulary

Assuming that your story now isn't a thinly disguised ad, let's add some other rules to help your news stories look professional.

The most common mistake, other than too many adjectives and unqualified puffery, is the use of hifalutin words. Some people foam at the mouth when they sit at the typewriter. They'll take out a dictionary and go out of their way to exhibit what they believe to be their erudition but what the reader either resents because he can't understand it or finds objectionable because he recognizes it as pomposity.

Here are a few obfuscations (words that obscure meaning) detected (seen) in representative (typical) news release composition (writing):

Why say:	when you can say:
eschew	*avoid?*
postulate	*claim?*
edifice	*building?*
megalopolis	*city?*
malcontent	*dissatisfied?*
declaim	*speak?*
pronounce	*say?*
adjudication	*judgment?*

You may never use any of these words, but the chances are that you have some pet multisyllabic constructions that nonplus your peruser.

If there is any rule for word use, it is this: Your purpose is to communicate, not to show off your vocabulary.

Assuring Accuracy

Another rule for writing news releases is to be slavishly dedicated to accuracy. Ask any editor. He'll tell you how many releases he discards because of misspelled words and missing or half-stated facts. Some stories misspell the senders' own name. Some spell the city wrong.

Next to misspelled words, the most objectionable inaccuracy is the unproved claim ("oldest car dealership in the city"; "largest department store in the state"; "most important real estate development in years"). If your car dealership is the oldest, name the date of establishment. If yours is the largest department store in the state, give an impartial reference to prove it, unless its reputation makes proof unnecessary.

Part of the problem isn't really inaccuracy; it's the use of superlatives. Use of words such as *oldest, largest, best,* and *most* represents claim rather than fact, and there is danger in unproved claims.

Another inaccuracy is poor structure or grammar. If you tend to tie two sentences together with commas, or if you write "It is me" and "They gave it to you and I," have someone more conversant with proper grammar proofread your copy before submission. A news release that runs in its entirety represents the newspaper, not you. Poor grammar reflects on the newspaper's literacy as well as yours, which means a double risk: the publication may reject the release; and if it runs, readers will criticize it.

Another problem is lack of specificity. This pertains to the information in the news story itself. Too often, this lack is the result of nothing but laziness. The writer will say "next week" when he should specify, "July 15." He'll say "of recent date" instead of "last August." If you remember that puff is no substitute for facts, you'll gradually discipline yourself to take the time to get those facts.

Format

All news releases are typed and double-spaced. No exceptions.

Refer to the formats in the second appendix. The sender's

name, address, and phone number are typed in the upper right-hand corner. If the sender is corporate, a contact name appears so that an editor looking for additional facts, clarification, or even a longer story will have a specific person to call.

The spacing between the top of the sheet and the beginning of the story allows the newspaper copy desk to indicate the headline. Reporters hand in their own stories that way, and copyreaders are used to it. They *can* clip a separate sheet to your story, but they won't want to. Since you're begging for space, play it their way.

Four spaces before the beginning of the story, type the release information, in capital letters and underlined. Usually the wording is:

FOR IMMEDIATE RELEASE

But this is by no means the only possibility. You're telling the media when the story is valid. It's entirely conceivable that your story will be headed:

FOR RELEASE 10 AM, MONDAY, AUGUST 15, 1977

This might be to coincide with the delivery of new models, to coordinate with national news, to time financial information, or to avoid the embarrassment of overlapping stories. Don't use that kind of timing unless it has some significance. It could result in the story's being shelved and forgotten.

You also might note exclusivity in the release information:

SPECIAL TO BAKERS WEEKLY

EXCLUSIVE TO "OUR TOWN" COLUMN

Appearance

All news stories should be typed on 8½-by-11-inch white paper. Never use onionskin paper.

There was a time when every company had its own news

release form with "NEWS!" in 120-point type printed in red across the top. Or, in two or three colors, up to half the first sheet would have corporate logos and seals and "IMPOR-TANT NEWS FROM THE XYZ CORPORATION."

Press-agentry in dealing with media is of dubious worth. The circus approach suggests an unpleasant fact—it's true, but we shouldn't go out of our way to emphasize it—which is that the information on that sheet isn't news but flackery. It's an approach out of key with today's serious public relations marketplace.

Copies should be made on a photocopy machine that produces sharp blacks and whites (the grainy gray copies are okay for office use but not for professional submission), or they should be mimeographed or sent to an instant printer for copying. Ditto copies are not acceptable—a regrettable fact because the machine is so easy to use. And carbon copies should never be submitted. A carbon copy is an insult to the person receiving it.

Leave ample margins on both sides. This makes editorial notes, changes, and corrections possible. Use only one side of the paper. If your release runs more than a page, type "more" at the bottom of each page except the last.

At the end of the story, use any of these:

— END —

# # #

— 30 —

The "30" is obsolete but still used by some old-timers. As an opinion: it marks you as out of touch with reality.

Style

If your story is being sent to one medium only, check their normal style. Do they capitalize such titles as "president" and "chairperson"? Do they use numerals or spell out numbers? Do they say "Mr. Jones" or just "Jones" in personal references after the first mention? Your story should follow that style.

If your publication is being sent to several outlets, here are some general rules of style that can apply to most news releases:

1. Spell out numbers from one to ten, then use numerals for 11 or more.

2. Never begin a sentence with a number.

3. Don't use "Mr." before a man's full name. In referring to a married woman, use "Mrs." and her husband's name (Mrs. Robert Smith) and "Mrs." and her last name thereafter (Mrs. Smith). Unmarried women may be referred to without title in a first reference (Mary Smith), and "Miss" and the last name are used subsequently (Miss Smith). Widows remain "Mrs. Robert Smith"; divorced women usually prefer their own first names: "Mrs. Mary Smith." Modern usage makes it logical and convenient to refer to *all* women in women's-lib fashion: "Mary Smith" the first time, then "Ms. Smith." Children should be referred to by full name in a first reference, then usually by their first names.

4. Capitalize titles when they precede a name (*President John Jones*); use lower case when the title follows the name (*John Jones, president of . . .*).

Photos

Not long ago the image of a news photo was tied to another image: a maniac photographer with hatbrim turned up and Speed Graphic in hand, elbowing and shoving and leaving a trail of used flashbulbs in his wake. The very existence of the Speed Graphic, with its hand-loaded four-by-five inch plates, implied that only the superpros had better try taking pictures for the newspapers.

Today's cameras, with built-in exposure meters and self-firing stroboscopic lights, and today's fine-grain films mean that only a need for extraordinary speed necessitates the issuance of a news story without accompanying photographs. Even Polaroid shots frequently appear in print.

Why aren't more news releases accompanied by photographs? The answer is cost—but this argument is specious when one considers the cost (and the purpose) of the news release the photograph might illustrate. The real answer is that it's too much trouble.

The fact is that sending a photograph with a cutline instead of a news release might well result in greater coverage. The news outlet might not look at your news release; you know they'll look at your photograph.

The Mechanics of Photographs. Until the 1960s, eight-by-ten inch prints were *de rigueur.* Today, the less expensive and easier-to-handle five-by-seven prints are accepted on equal terms. The eight-by-ten size is impressive, but chances are that the publication will reproduce that photograph far smaller than five-by-seven.

One requirement hasn't changed. Prints should be glossy, not matte. This is because glossy prints usually are sharper, improving reproduction quality.

Horizontal photographs—that is, photographs made with a 35mm camera in normal position—usually are preferable to vertical. Turning the camera sideways to make a "tall" or vertical shot is common for buildings or for full-length shots of individuals.

Cropping is important. Usually, having shot a twenty- or thirty-six-exposure roll of 35mm black-and-white film, you'll receive back from the laboratory a proof sheet—contact prints of each shot, printed on one or two eight-by-ten sheets.

Having chosen the photograph or photographs you want to use, check them carefully for *cropping.* Does something show that you don't want to show? Have you made too wide a shot? Put crop marks on the proof; the laboratory will follow those marks in making quantity prints.

If you're setting up head-and-shoulders shots, perhaps of key personnel, remember that the difference between professional and amateur photographs often is nothing other than a rim light—a photoflood bulb above and behind the subject, adding a pleasing edge to the hair and shoulder line.

Avoid faces in the dark. Avoid large black areas. Avoid shooting into shadows.

Composition.   What you should avoid most of all is dullness. The purpose of including photographs is to make the story more interesting. Have you done that if your photograph shows two men standing uncomfortably side by side or shaking hands?

Use all your ingenuity to think of ways to avoid the deadly handshake. If two companies merge, what's the picture? The two presidents shaking hands. Again. A better shot might show one president turning over the keys to the other (if the company is progressive and promotion-minded, you might be able to say that one of them is the key to the executive washroom). Or take a shot of the two men symbolically pushing their chairs together or painting the first letter of the new corporate name on the front door or inspecting a "wedding cake" that has figures of two buildings or two symbols of the kinds of businesses. Any of these has a better chance of being printed, because any of these is superior to a handshake.

Another classic example of the dull photograph is the groundbreaking ceremony. Holding a golden shovel, the head of the company turns over the first spadeful of earth. Better would be to have that president operate a bulldozer or a steamshovel. Even though his hand is guided by the normal operator, the action shot is less phony and hackneyed than the one editors refer to as "the golden shovel bit."

4
psychological tools: awards and celebrities

If the business person, the head of an organization, or the appointed "publicity chairperson" is to function in more than a perfunctory way, he or she should think beyond the basic submission of news releases to media. Using psychological tools is well within the capability of anyone who wants to go beyond the basics.

The one rule that might apply to the methods described in this chapter is: don't get too complicated.

Giving and Receiving Awards

An award is a symbol of achievement, and awards always build image and always are good reasons for news releases.

Obviously the best awards are those given to you by an outside, nonpartisan source, but these represent only one kind of award. There are others, easily controlled, that can represent a regular facet of your public relations activities. A few of them are described in this chapter.

Giving an award is substantially easier to arrange than receiving an award, since all one needs in order to proceed is the agreement of the recipient to accept the award. While it is more blessed to receive than to give, peculiar benefits accrue to the person or company who gives an award. Chief benefit is that when one individual gives an award to another, he is implicitly in a position superior to that of the one receiving it.

What reason might a businessman have for giving an award? Here are the four main areas of award-giving in which one normally might participate:

1.   Give an award for community service. Worthy candidates for this kind of award seem to abound. Advance publicity is relatively easy to accomplish as you ask for nominations; follow-up publicity is as logical as the award itself.

2.   Give an award for industry service. This award can be a vertical award, to someone within your own field of business or industry. If the award can be given at a major industry function or convention, extra importance means extra public relations value.

3.   Give a special recognition award to someone who has accomplished something truly worthy of recognition. Someone who has given a lifetime of service to a business or community is your logical candidate.

4.   Give an award totally unrelated to your business. The award can be an annual award at a local art fair, a high school essay contest award (obvious prize: a scholarship to a college), a best-of-parade award for the Fourth of July parade, or an achievement award to volunteers of any local civic club or group.

Intramural Awards.   Intramural awards are those you decide to give within your own company or organization. Since you initiate the awards, you control both timing and rationale.

Reasons for intramural awards should not be capricious.

They should make sense within the structure of the group. For example, you can give awards to divisions or departments for efficiency, output, or sales increases, or you can have annual awards—the President's Award or the Annual Division Award.

One-shot awards can be given to individuals for a singular achievement—perhaps a civic act not directly related to business (such as unselfish dedication of time to a civic or charitable cause), an unusually profitable suggestion made to the company itself, or a personal achievement worthy of note (publication of a book or an article in a periodical, a sports victory, or longevity on the job).

A third category of intramural award is the memorial or "in-the-name-of" award, given once a year with considerable fanfare to the one employee who has done the most to—whatever. To validate this award, the company should ask outsiders to judge entries submitted by employees. If this panel of judges includes people from media, the public relations function is built in.

Awards for sportsmanship, good fellowship, popularity, and efficiency can be given in the memory of a company founder or a well-known officer or department head whose name carries an association of dignity or even reverence. (The Irving Thalberg Award at the annual motion picture Academy Awards is a prime example of the "in memoriam" award.) In addition to honoring the person for whom the award is named, the award gradually becomes an accepted annual recognition worthy of media coverage. A chamber of commerce Joe Jones Award for community service, a country club Bill Nagle Award for the best-natured golfer, and the Brown Construction Company's Herman Brown Award for the most constructive attitude all are pressworthy annual awards.

Obviously, a company with four employees cannot use intramural awards extensively without seeming silly to both media and the public. Such a ploy is simply an obtrusive attempt to gain publicity. But the company with a dozen or more employees gains more than public notice from an awards program; internally, a separate public relations function is served (see Chapter 7).

What should the award be? A certificate, plaque, or trophy should accompany any other gift. In some cases, the certificate, plaque, or trophy is all you may need. These are familiar to all media, and no photographer will have any question of procedure when he is asked to take a picture of the presentation.

Typical intramural awards are a vacation trip, a cash bonus, a weekend for two at a resort, or a mini-banquet or luncheon. Psychological income is important, sometimes more important than the nominal amount of cash that might be possible within the small corporate structure.

Media may not cover the award presentation if they regard the event as too trivial. This is of less consequence than you might imagine if you have a photographer on hand to record the event and to make prints for subsequent distribution. Awards are strong contenders for space in local and trade media, and the fact that a newspaper won't send a crew to cover your intramural award doesn't mean your story won't be printed.

Remember that the purpose of the award is threefold: (1) to offer recognition to those who have given service, (2) to maintain a continuing internal public relations program, and (3) to achieve press coverage as part of a continuing external public relations program.

The suggestion box is a common stimulus for intramural awards. The suggestion box (sometimes a decorated rural-type mailbox) is placed in a prominent location, and employees are invited to submit suggestions for improving any aspect of the operation. While every suggestion box regularly yields unsigned obscenities and wisecracks, management that shows serious consideration of serious suggestions soon finds that more and more such suggestions are submitted. Awards should be publicized within the organization as well as externally, and monthly or quarterly awards can be precursors of an annual award.

Association Awards. Association awards are given by a group of affiliates to one of their number. Every industry has an association, and every association should sponsor awards. If yours doesn't, you can make it start by suggestion, action, and implementation. As prime mover, you may well control the award machinery.

As with all positive public relations programs, success in award-receiving is no accident. Suppose you're a member of an association that simply never has given awards. Suggest (and, if necessary, form) an awards committee. If the association is dead set against awards (which they might be out of fear of anger from nonrecipients) and if you are unable to convince the group of the public relations merit of award-giving, you have these choices:

1. Forget the matter;
2. Sponsor an award that you give *outside* the structure of the organization;
3. Organize a members' committee to sponsor an award;
4. Start another association.

In militating for an awards program, you have one major asset: Most members couldn't care less; you do. This is automatic assurance that your viewpoint will prevail.

If you're responsible for setting up an awards program, be sure to have multiple awards. You can't head the program and use it to give yourself the only award. But you can be one of five, which is ample for your personal public relations program.

One way of implementing awards is to ask for candidates. This at once cuts the competition, because ordinary indolence will eliminate many and false modesty will kill off most of the rest. Only those hardy battlers as aggressive as you will apply.

The application for awards should consist of two components: a questionnaire and exhibits. Suppose that yours is a retail operation. The award might be for most professional display, best sales promotion activity, or best community relations. The questionnaire asks for a factual description of the circumstances; the exhibits include photographs, samples, printed news releases, comments from the community or suppliers, and other verification. Those who regularly issue awards must agree that attention is indeed paid to bulk. Amassing a host of exhibits is one way to assure yourself of one award or another, since quantity cannot be ignored. The exhibits say, "We seriously think we deserve to win."

If you are on the judging committee and your own entry surfaces, you say, "Fellows, you'll have to judge this award without me, because I'm fighting for this one." The remark alone might well make you a popular favorite, but don't count on an automatic victory unless your exhibits indicate that you seriously believe you deserve the award.

Media Awards.   Media awards are given by advertising media —newspapers, broadcast stations, magazines, and (most important) trade papers. If you're a consistent advertiser in a publication that serves the community or the trade, suggest to the space salesman who calls on you that he either ask his sales promotion or advertising manager to set up an awards program or else make an appointment for you to discuss such a program. Obviously, if a logical medium already gives an award, compete for it.

The advantage of an award given by an advertising medium is that the announcement of the award means automatic news coverage within that medium. Media can give awards not only for community or intra-industry service but also for excellence in any aspect of the business enterprise itself—

efficiency, salesmanship, statesmanship, leadership, or any combination of these, within many categories of size and dollar volume.

Like awards from associations, awards from media need not be exclusive. Yours may be one of five or ten or twenty. The difference, hopefully, is that where competitors may accept the award graciously, you accept the award graciously *and* exploit the daylights out of the award in your own public relations program.

Awards from Suppliers. Awards from suppliers are the easiest to arrange, since suppliers not only want your goodwill but will be grateful for means of cementing a relationship with you. But one warning: *do something* to make the award look and be deserved.

Chances are that a supplier won't at first have any idea what you're talking about when you say, "Joe, I want you to give us the first annual Smith Plastics Company Award for Best Sales Promotion." As he recovers from his bewilderment, he may well comment that it's relatively unethical and also dangerous to his relationship with other customers. This is why you should not ask for an award only because you're a good customer; you should ask because you're a good customer *and* because you deserve it.

Actually, under the rules of this chapter, issuing awards will benefit your supplier in his own public relations miniprogram. But if you baldly approach a supplier with a demand for a certificate, trophy, or plaque, be prepared to temper the demand with concessions: yours will be the award for the northeastern states with others awarded in other regions; or yours will be limited to your own industry with others possible in other industries; or you have no objection to competitors being given similar awards if their achievements equal yours in the areas of competition for which the award is given.

In many areas of commerce and industry, associations,

media, and suppliers have active awards programs. To compete, all you need to do is take them seriously and start sending in entries. Veteran judges agree that few entrants make more than perfunctory efforts in pursuit of the awards they might win by a more organized entry, the one exception being (not so oddly) awards given by publicity or public relations clubs to members for their own efforts—awards that are fought for with life-or-death grimness by applicants within a not-very-gentlemanly profession.

Obviously, you're in a better position if a third party recommends you for an award than if you try to arrange it for yourself. The third party can be an employee, a business associate, your advertising agency, a friend, or—best of all—someone in a position to influence the giver. Similarly, if you are planning to give an award, a third person can eliminate any embarrassment, since a negative reaction will be blunted by the buffer person.

One major word of warning is in order relative to receiving or giving an award: It is easy to lapse into cynicism, viewing awards *solely* as publicity generators. Don't do it. Give awards sincerely; receive them graciously; do both for good cause and purpose. The publicity that inevitably ensues is then deserved by you and accepted by your contemporaries.

The Care and Feeding of Celebrities

What would you do with a celebrity if you had one? In our strange society in which celebrities are lionized because they're celebrities (one astute comment: "A celebrity is someone well known for his well-knownness"), they become useful to the businessman who either wants an association on which he can coattail-ride or who wants the automatic press coverage (especially outside the top ten markets) that comes with having a celebrity on hand.

While most celebrities come from show business, increasing numbers come from sports. Politics yields a group who regard themselves as celebrities, who qualify as celebrities because of their continuous exposure through electronic media, and who want any kind of exposure as long as it's free. And a cadre whose significance in the ranks of celebrities has leaped in the past several years comes from the field of literature. The anonymous, mousy author of twenty years ago has been replaced by the photogenic, freewheeling male or female authors of the 1970s who take their places alongside actors and actresses in the celebrity sweepstakes.

Research has shown that some sports personalities have negative public relations value. This is especially true of boxers and hockey and football players. Baseball players and golfers are regarded as relatively safe, and tennis is too new a source of celebrities for a generalized conclusion to be drawn.

Under what circumstances might you want a celebrity on hand? You might want one to add a name for a grand opening, a banquet, or an awards ceremony, or for product introduction.

Half a dozen major companies and any number of smaller ones deal in celebrities for a price. Some specialize only in sports figures or literary names or film/television faces. All will offer you a selection based on your budget or will negotiate with a specific "name" you might want. If you have no idea where or how to find a celebrity, contact a local talent agency or models' bureau. They'll know where to look— for a 10 percent fee for themselves.

The going price for the appearance of a nationally recognizable celebrity is $500 to $5,000, plus transportation and lodging. The most celebrated of celebrities probably are not available at all within the budget range of the typical businessman. In the off season, sports celebrities may be available for several months to accompany a touring trade show or to help with product introductions in several areas. Purely *local* celebrities, such as disc jockeys, columnists, rock or folk musicians, and politicians, may cost only $100—or nothing at all if the media coverage seems ample enough to offer them ego income.

Suppose you've negotiated with one of the national sources of celebrities-for-a-price. You have Joe Jones, "the popular emcee of that famous quiz show . . . ," as your man to help introduce your new line of merchandise. How much of his time can you commandeer, and what might you expect him to do within the framework of the agreement?

Since Joe Jones undoubtedly never heard of you before, don't expect your dynamic personality to overwhelm him and turn him into a slathering booster. He's enough of a pro not to look completely bored, but he's mercenary enough to do exactly what he's agreed to do and mutter, "See my agent," if you want him to do more. So it's important to include in the original agreement his appearance at one major news conference and, say, three interviews—perhaps one each for a television show, a radio show (preferably morning time), and a newspaper feature or financial writer. You might also ask that Jones be available for meals with customers or clients. And you might ask that he arrive the night before in order to make a breakfast session. This serves two purposes. First, you can use that breakfast to brief Jones on yourself, your product, and what he might say that will be helpful. Second, you can rest easier the night before, knowing that Jones is in town and that whatever goes wrong on the big day, there won't be the handwringing cry, "What happened to Jones?"

You have Jones for the whole day until you pour him onto a plane back to California at 10 P.M. The temptation is to milk every minute he's on hand. But there are two reasons you shouldn't: (1) Jones simply isn't used to that kind of schedule; and (2) Jones will become so increasingly apathetic toward his job as the day continues that the impact will be the reverse of what you're trying to achieve.

If you have Jones for a single day, give him two two-hour breaks. If he's a true celebrity he'll know local people he wants to see or at least call, or he can change clothes or snooze. And he won't feel like a trained monkey.

But a worse mistake is to pussyfoot. Jones is to speak at the luncheon at 1 P.M. Through fear of waking him no one calls him until 11:30. Jones is picked up in the biggest, newest car anyone in the company owns and briefed on the way to the luncheon. He arrives after the others already have started eating—one of the worst mistakes you can make when you know that many have come only to shake hands with Jones. Then, immediately after concluding his prefabricated Robert Benchley stump speech, he is driven to the airport, where even before his plane takes off he has forgotten you and who it was he spoke to that day.

Whatever the schedule, leave "socializing time" so those for whom you've spent the money to bring in Jones can have a chance to talk with him and get the feeling he's "your man." Anyone who wants to should be able to go home and say, "I met Joe Jones today, Martha. He's a pretty good guy."

Beware of subsequent legal problems. Jones has agreed to appear at the opening of your store. The written contract clearly gives you the right to publicize his appearance and to take photographs. But how may you use those photographs? It's unlikely that you can use his picture in your ads weeks after he has come and gone. To do so without prior agreement can lead to embarrassment and legal action. Be sure to clarify the relationship in a written agreement. It might be that Jones won't permit the use of his name as an endorsement but that Smith, who's every bit as big a celebrity as Jones, will.

Many car dealers will give a professional athlete free use of a car in exchange for an endorsement. Included might be the right to use the name in ads and a guarantee of half a dozen showroom appearances during the season. Before using this method, weigh carefully the credibility factor of the celebrity. In the Age of Skepticism, is it truly worthwhile? Perhaps it is, but not always.

Since we're in the Age of Skepticism, why use a celebrity? Here are four main public relations reasons for considering this avenue of sales promotion:

1.   Using celebrities means automatic news media coverage. An identical event without the celebrity can result in no coverage whatever through lack of a news "handle."

2.   Celebrities have better public acceptance than company officials. Sure, everyone knows you've paid for the appearance and/or the endorsement. Sure, everyone knows that celebrities are for sale. But a celebrity often is important enough to ask for an autograph; a company officer isn't.

3.   Even though everyone knows it's a commercial venture, the public accepts the event as more important if a celebrity is on hand. The sense of importance is contagious: "If they think it's a big enough deal to have Joe Jones on hand, it must be a big deal."

4.   The celebrity adds mileage to the event. His pictures with company people are grist for the house organ; visits to dealers or outside locations add a dimension to the corporate relationship; and it's possible to achieve coverage from columnists and broadcast personalities who otherwise never touch hard business coverage.

As more and more businessmen become conscious of public relations and publicity, we may expect the use of celebrities to increase. Certainly, between 1966 and 1976, the increase was somewhere between 500 and 1,000 percent, and there seems to be no slackening off despite the gradual narrowing of the sophistication gap between celebrities and the rest of us. Celebrities do make sense as a weapon in the public relations arsenal. But, like any dangerous weapon, they should be handled with care.

5   **outlets**

Newspapers

For pure publicity on the local level, newspapers are your best hope for success, largely because the demand for information to fill a newspaper is insatiable. Each day, each week, the newspaper gobbles up press handouts together with news from its own sources, prints them, and begins to look for more. A broadcast station may have newscasts every hour, but these have few holes since the most important national and local news must be repeated in each newscast.

Departmentalization. Large daily newspapers are so departmentalized that many editorial personnel may scarcely know each other. Deciding to whom a news release should be sent often is as critical as the content of the release itself. A few major categories of departments, each with its own editor and staff are: News (city desk), Sports, Women's/Fashion/Society, Food, Amusements/Entertainment, Travel, Financial, Features, Photos, Weekend magazine, Columnists.

The businessman usually thinks in terms of business, so his information is sent to the financial editor. Yet often he has a stronger shot at a different readership. For example, suppose that you are the processor of an ethnic food—packaged tortillas. Your volume is up 200 percent. There is no question that this is a business item; but there is no question, either, that the better way of handling this information is to *interpret*. The demand for tortillas means that they're selling in the non-ethnic marketplace. The food editor might welcome this information, together with some recipes using tortillas. The financial release provides some self-aggrandizement; the food release might mean another jump in sales.

The Contact List. Every public relations professional not only maintains a contact list; he fights to keep it current, and he guards it as he would gold against a competitor's copying it.

The contact list isn't that complicated. It's nothing more than a list of press contacts. Who's the right man at the *Daily News*? How about the same paper, financial department? Who's the proper contact or the stringer for the Associated Press or United Press International? Who at television station WXXX decides whether a newsreel crew will be sent out or not? Who's the fashion editor of the weekly shopper? Who's the lively arts editor of the high school newspaper?

In smaller communities, the list may be short. For a businessman whose prospective outlets are regional, national, or international rather than local, the contact list may have a hundred names or more. The old-time publicity man had *everyone* on his list. He easily could send out "comps" (complimentary tickets) to five hundred people for a theatrical preview. (NOTE: filling a theatre with comps is generally called "papering the house.")

At Christmas, everyone on the contact list gets a card.

(*Better:* send a sincere thank-you at Thanksgiving, when the mail isn't full of competing messages.) I've seen many a case of scotch, hi-fi sets, and even more expensive gifts sent to a benefactor on a contact list by a grateful public relations (publicity) man.

Using the Phone. You're dealing with professional writers when you submit news releases to a newspaper. Occasionally it pays to phone first, especially in the following circumstances:

1. You're offering an exclusive.
2. You're extending an invitation and requesting a definite reply.
3. You want to introduce yourself so that your news release doesn't arrive "cold."
4. You want to make an appointment to bring a sample or to hand deliver the news release or to offer a choice of photographs.
5. You want to learn something—the right name or the hours that person is in the office.

Some newspaper people sound unnecessarily curt on the phone. There can be many reasons—they're busy; they hate news handouts in general; they have the arrogance that grows like fungus on many members of the fourth estate. Expect rudeness now and then, but don't blow your cool. They have a newspaper; you don't.

Don't phone on impulse. Have an outline at least; this will prevent a rambling, disconnected, or incoherent conversation that would exasperate even the most patient listener. Think in terms of yourself. Don't *you* appreciate a crisp, businesslike, organized, *brief* call?

Here is one last tip, perhaps most important of all. It's a basic law of salesmanship that when the person you've called says yes, get off the phone as fast as you can.

Success with Newspapers. When you submit a news release, use the format prescribed in Chapter 3. If you're gunning for a specific day's paper, think in terms of deadlines. When does the paper close? Many morning papers have their first editions on the street at 5:30 P.M. the previous evening. Obviously, a release that hits an editor in the early afternoon catches him at "prime" time. But it's also his busiest time. An afternoon paper usually prints its first edition at 9:30 or 10:00 A.M. Much of its content is determined the day before, in the late afternoon.

Weekly papers usually appear Thursday or Friday. Even though they "close" Monday or Tuesday, never push a deadline with weekly newspapers. They fill their pages by the accretion method, and often the best day is the day after the previous issue was published, so that your story is in the first batch. Once set in type, chances of its appearance are excellent, since to set it and not use it is a waste of money that papers like to avoid.

It's my opinion (and the basis for professional argument, I know) that in a community of ten thousand to fifty thousand persons that has its own weekly paper anyone who has any writing ability or the money to hire a "ghost writer," plus a strong desire, should be able to negotiate a column of one sort or another for himself or herself. The paper may not pay you, but they'll accept the column *provided* it isn't self-puffery, or loaded with fustian (look it up), or downright dull—which it can't be if you know what communicates and what doesn't.

Here are some areas in which you can submit sample columns *tomorrow*:

Dramatic Criticism	Reviews of New Recordings
Eating Out	Gossip
Golf, Tennis, Skiing	Travel
History of the Community	Beautiful Homes
High School News or Sports	Recipes
Local Business Trends	"Man about Town."

Don't expect to walk into the offices of the *New York*

Times and demand to be appointed their art critic. You need some credentials and background; but your sample columns for a local newspaper may well provide those, and other questions won't be asked if your writing is bright, entertaining, and reader-oriented.

On the local level, editors aren't used to dogged determination, and when for six weeks in a row an "eating out" column (which doesn't attack advertisers) is submitted, each one at least as well written as staff articles, an editor is likely to start printing them.

This is where the "be-the-first-on-your-block" principle applies, because a newspaper will not throw out an existing column in favor of a new one. Read the paper carefully and justify what you're writing in terms of *reader interest, not your own.*

WARNING: Don't believe for one minute that *desire* to write a column is equivalent to *ability* to write a column. Your work must be competitive, professional, entertaining, and informative. If it isn't, drop the idea or hire someone to do it for you (which admittedly *isn't* being your own public relations person).

Don't make a career of cultivating editors. Regard it as just another implement of marketing, and you won't lose your perspective—or your sense of humor.

Magazines and Special Readership Publications

Most categorizers divide magazines into two groups—consumer and trade—with farm publications sometimes listed as "special interest" consumer/trade magazines.

In an era when electronic media coupled with newspaper use of features and continuing consumer sophistication have driven many of the once-mighty consumer publications out of business (*Life, Look, Collier's,* and hundreds more), the "special interest" appellation today applies to most consumer magazines as well as trade publications. A magazine is a men's magazine (*Playboy, Esquire*) or a women's magazine (*Glamour, Cosmopolitan*) or a sports magazine (*Sports Illustrated, Field & Stream*) or a news magazine (*Time, Newsweek*) or a business magazine (*Fortune, Forbes*) or a religious magazine (*Extension, Commentary*), or it fits into another category that describes a selective area of interest—a "vertical" special interest rather than a "horizontal" general interest.

Obviously, magazines such as *Iron Age* or *Meetings & Conventions* or the *Journal of the American Medical Association* are more vertical in selectivity of their reader-interest groups, but the heavy line that once differentiated consumer from trade magazines no longer exists. Some trade magazines are, if anything, sprightlier in format and easier to read than the more ponderous consumer publications.

Before you submit anything to a magazine, however, *learn something about it.* I wish I had a nickel—even a penny —for every unsolicited manuscript sent to a magazine that under no circumstances could use it. I'd settle for one mill for every photograph sent to a magazine that could never, within its format, accept that photograph.

Obviously, if you are a mortician, you should know the general editorial requirements of *American Funeral Director*. But, as the examples in Chapter 10 point out, funeral directors are *local*—they would benefit little from national exposure, unless that exposure were geared to a major recognition on which the individual might capitalize locally.

But suppose you're not a mortician, but a supplier. You manufacture an artificial grass that, among its many other uses, can be used at graveside. In order to publicize your product, you prepare a news release, with appropriate photographs, and send the packet off to all the undertakers' publications you can find. That release could be written by Joseph Pulitzer or Aldous Huxley, but if it doesn't match the publication, it just won't be printed.

Television

Because television is the newest and most glamorous medium, the one that can bring instant fame, it quickly has become the most overapproached and misunderstood of all media.

Appearances on television carry with them exposure to the most advantageous and the most dangerous aspects of the Age of Skepticism. Many a businessman, finally realizing his dream of becoming an instant celebrity on television, "chokes," lapses into nervous giggles, talks too much and/or too fast, or tries to lecture a talk show host. The result is ridicule rather than adulation.

But how does one get to the point where he at least has the opportunity to make a jackass of himself in front of the color cameras? The most obvious way is to negotiate for an invitation to be interviewed. And there are three steps to take in order to make this happen:

1. Make a list of everyone on the air locally who might invite you on the show for any reason.

2. Figure out a reason for yourself to be interviewed.

3. Call, or have an associate call, the producer of the shows, one by one, to try to spark an interest.

Here's what you have going for you: the insatiable maw of television gobbles up program material. You manufacture buttonhole-making machines. This talk show has had every show business personality, every local politician, and every visiting fireman, and a week from Tuesday there's no one booked. You, or the person riding shotgun for you, suggests to the producer that you can show some interesting ways of making buttonholes, will have some clever cartoons showing the history of buttonholes, and will briefly discuss how buttonholes influence fashion.

Or suppose you're an insurance broker; what could be duller? But you offer the producer of a women's show your comments on "Equal Insurance Opportunities for Women"; you suggest to a sports commentator that you're available to discuss special and novel insurance for athletes; you offer the host of an ethnic job market or commentary show a rare potential treat: an expert will appear on the show, describing job opportunities in insurance. When national or even local news suggests an increase in premiums for some types of insurance, you're the one who volunteers to supply a local angle.

Personal appearances are only one way of using television. A manufacturer, distributor, or dealer can supply silent color footage to news departments with suggested commentary. This works especially well in areas that have automatic change, such as fashion, automobiles, sports equipment, shoes, hi-fi and recording equipment, seasonal foods, building products, and travel.

Newsreel footage supplied to stations also is a logical move for builders, for anyone introducing a new product, and for food stores offering menu-planning suggestions. In each case, if footage is used once with positive viewer response, the second submission is accepted far more easily.

Standard for television film footage is 16mm color film, perforated on one edge only. Since most film that goes through the camera is "double-perf" with holes on both sides, this means making prints with a blacked-off sound track. If someone in the station's control room inadvertently leaves the sound level at its normal position, double-perf film will create an annoying popping sound until the sound is turned down; single-perf film will run through with no sound.

Occasionally someone will supply a television station with super-8mm film. Through a series of special hookups, it is perhaps possible for some stations to project the film. But super-8 is not only a variation from the norm; it's not considered professional film.

For videotape, two-inch high-band tape is standard. Some stations can handle one-inch tape. The half-inch and quarter-inch tape that home videotape units use are incompatible with television station equipment.

Stations also are geared to project 35mm slides. For television use, the slides should be glass-mounted, to assure proper seating in the station's projectors.

Other visuals, such as title cards and photographic prints, can be picked up by studio cameras. Don't offer too extraordinary a challenge to the small station that may produce an entire show using a single camera armed only with a zoom lens.

Calling a news conference may bring out the television crews. As described in Chapter 6, this is a sophisticated public relations technique that can backfire if improperly handled.

The one great coup that occasionally is brought off is persuading a station's program manager to make you a regular—perhaps on a sports show as the expert in fishing or skiing, on a women's show as the expert in buttonhole sewing, on a news show as the drama-critic-in-residence, or on a cooking show as the expert in desserts, budget cookery, available vegetables, or cuts of meat.

If you or what you do is invited to appear on television, think visually. If you're thoughtful enough to bring some props, some photographs, some film footage, or a demonstration that departs from the look of a radio show with pictures, you're a hero both in the studio and on the home screens.

Radio

Of all media, radio offers the best opportunity for an individual to achieve exposure and recognition. It is a highly personal medium in which *personality* is as important as information, and its changing nature plus the multiplicity of competitors striving for public attention means that the individual who really wants exposure and whose ideas match the medium can be heard on the air.

This is not to suggest that one can approach a major network outlet and immediately be assigned a show of his own.

It does mean that, within the framework of news and features, one can become *the* person called to comment on news pertinent to his field.

One method is to tape some comments and carry or send the tape to each station in turn, starting with the station you would most like to be on and ending with the lowest-wattage or least important FM station. Somewhere down the line, assuming that your comments are at all valid, your search stops. Program directors are looking for fresh material, provided that material fits the station's format.

Suppose you are in the retail clothing business. You tape a five-minute commentary on fashion. Your comments are pleasant, humorous, biting, dryly informative—whatever matches your personality and delivery. One station or another will be interested on a daily, semiweekly, or weekly basis— *provided your commentary is professional and interesting and matches the listenership pattern of the station's audience.*

If you're in the theater business, offer movie reviews. Even though both network and syndicated reviews are available, the station will lean toward your reviews if they're entertaining and not self-serving.

If you're an accountant, lawyer, or doctor, offer a tape-recorded commentary on taxes, legal problems, or medicine, emphasizing local situations or problems.

If you're in the automobile, appliance, grocery, or furniture business, offer a weekly commentary on how to keep your car running well, how to save electricity, what the best food buys are, and how to decorate the home.

If yours is a business that does not deal directly with the public (that is, an industrial or commercial enterprise), offer commentaries on business conditions.

Obviously, this isn't simple or easy. It would be both cynical and foolish to believe that all one need do is decide he is worthy of air time and station programming departments will fall all over themselves to get him on the air. As with all logical and thoughtful public relations projects, the method itself is logical and thoughtful. Achieving on-the-air exposure is the result of listening to what other people want to hear and adapting the message to what they want.

One exception is if you tell the station that you're prepared to sponsor the show commercially. Chances are then that you'll have a taker—perhaps not the best station in town but one of the hungrier stations. And you yourself need not be the sponsor. You might persuade a businessman (an acquaintance or even a total stranger) to pay for air time and a modest talent fee. The combination of decent programming and commercial sponsorship often is irresistible.

Panel discussions offer another avenue for on-the-air exposure. Many stations have no such programs; in such cases, you might, if you are well connected, offer to produce one. The station might well assign a "ghetto" time to the show for starters, but you can use the vehicle as a springboard to better time or even better stations. And you can make many excellent contacts by inviting guests to appear on the program. It is somewhat arrogant, however, to think that you can walk in cold and be named producer of a discussion show. You must have a hard, valid idea and be able to prove that you can carry it off. To do this, you might enlist an academician or journalist as a partner. He or she would be the actual host of the show until your own name becomes better known and accepted.

If discussion shows do exist, call the producer and ask to be included on a future show. Suggest topics and controversy, and be sure to have some names of other people who might represent an opposing point of view. Thus you present a complete "package" or segment of a forthcoming show. Producers are likely to accept such a request, whereas they might well put off, shelve, or reject a flat request for on-the-air exposure without the suggestion of a proper vehicle.

News releases and prepared taped news are other means

of using radio stations for publicity and public relations.

To prepare taped material, the most common vehicle is a 7½-inch full-track quarter-inch tape for AM stations and a 7½-inch stereo tape for FM stations. More and more material is being submitted on cassettes; almost none uses the old "ETs" (electrical transcriptions), which were recorded discs. While the quarter-inch tape is usually a safe bet, it makes sense to call the station to learn what they're using. (This is a good way to make a first contact.)

When writing news releases for radio stations, be sure to remember that they're to be spoken aloud, not just read. This means that involved sentences and connecting words such as "which" should be avoided, as should words with more than one possible meaning or spelling: "It was red [read]"; "It became a principle [principal]"; "He could brake [break] easily."

Writing verbal material is easy. If you can say it without feeling it's stilted, write it that same way. A news release for print media might begin:

> Drew Bracken has been named head tennis professional at Highland Park Racquet Club. . . .

That same release, tailored for radio, might begin:

> There's a new head tennis pro at Highland Park Racquet Club. . . .

Write it the way you speak, and you'll have proper broadcast copy.

Speaking Engagements

Every community has clubs—civic, fraternal, scholastic, business, sports, common interest, and charitable. And when clubs meet, they often have as their principal entertainment an outside speaker. In many cases, becoming a luncheon or dinner speaker is no more difficult than making yourself available. Reading the newspapers daily will provide some of the club names. A phone call to the sales department of local meeting rooms, hotels, and restaurants will provide others.

Club news as reported in media usually includes a name or two of an officer of the club. A call to that individual will in turn bring you the name of the person responsible for the program. If you require no fee for your speech, you may well be manna to the harassed program chairman, whose source of speakers is limited because the broadcast personalities, celebrities, and politicians have been used up or are unavailable or too expensive and the secondary sources are thin.

Success in having yourself booked as a speaker lies in two tricks: the title of the speech and the promise of entertainment rather than a sermon. An architect found few takers for his speech "Architecture in Pakistan." But program chairmen did take a chance on "Those Crazy Pakistani Buildings," if only because the subject looked lively in newsletters to members. "Giants and Forty-Niners" seemed like a dull subject; "What's Wrong with San Francisco Teams?" did better in speech-booking. "How to Save Money on Taxes" wasn't bad but not as exciting as "Don't Let Uncle Sam Gyp You."

The actual technique of speechmaking is discussed in Chapter 9. Entertainment can be superimposed on a speech whether the speaker is polished or not. The simplest way is through the use of visuals—slides, film, or even large cards. When using visuals, be sure that they can be seen by everyone. Don't show up with equipment that will show only a two-foot-square picture for a slide-illustrated speech to a group of a hundred people.

Another simple way of adding a dimension of entertainment is to have questions popping from the audience. This is a comfortable procedure only if key questions are "salted" ahead of time with sympathetic friends in the group who will, on cue, ask the questions you have told them to ask.

Always remember, however, that the public relations function of a speech originates in its authoritarian content and not in its gimmicks. Unless you have a message to transmit, you're not qualified to approach a program chairman.

As is often the case in public relations, you may feel more comfortable about negotiating for a speech if you can have someone else make the first contact. This isn't always possible, but you're generally safe with this opening in a phone call: "Hello, Mr. Brown? My name is John Jones, and it's been suggested that I contact you about speaking before the Lackawanna Lions Club. I guess it's because of my speech, 'You're Paying Too Much in Taxes and I Can Prove It.' Are you interested in a speech like that?"

Even though the group has its own methods of publicizing the speech, once the booking is firm you might want to augment the news coverage. Some clubs publicize a speech only within their own membership. This may be of little value to you. Wait until the booking is firm and have your secretary call to ask whether the group has any objection to your answering a query about the speech from one of the news media. *Don't* start blowing your own horn until a contact with the group has been made, or you may find yourself in the embarrassing position of explaining away two separate sets of news releases, one from the group and one from you, that don't quite match.

Since one good speech tends to lead to another, treat yours seriously regardless of the group before which it's given. To do otherwise means the kind of speech that won't lead to another.

6 staged activities

The suggestions in this chapter are sophisticated, and for that very reason fewer of what you might consider your "competition" for print space and air time will use them.

The danger to a beginner is not in the approach; rather, it is in the method. Nothing in public relations is worse than appearing to be an amateur. Savoir faire and logic will do much to prevent amateurism in execution of the projects described in Chapter 6.

News Conferences

If any tool of public relations has been misunderstood and abused, it is the news conference, often called the "press conference."

A businessman sees a televised news conference held by the president of the United States, the governor of his state, or the developer who has announced construction of a $100 million domed sports complex. The next morning, he sees the coverage repeated in the newspaper and says, "That's for me!"

Misunderstanding and abuse tend to combine in business use of the news conference. At least half the problem stems from failure to observe this rule: *If the announcement can be made just as easily through a news release, don't hold a conference.*

Typically, a news conference is reserved for issues that contain one of these components: (1) controversy, (2) public interest, (3) announcement of a problem or its solution, (4) introduction of someone of consequence.

Thus, the conference is the proper vehicle to announce a strike or its settlement, construction of a major shopping center or housing development, appointment of the new football coach, or the decision to run for an important office. It is presumptuous to call a conference to announce just another real estate project or the appointment of a corporate vice president or the first public appearance of the new officers of a noncontroversial association.

Obviously there are borderline situations. New product introduction, mergers and major business transactions, and grand openings might or might not justify a conference, and perhaps it is unfair to discourage use of this device when it is indeed a most powerful public relations tool if used properly.

Because the consumer media dominate most people's attention, one may forget that it is possible and sensible to hold a news conference on the trade or industrial level. The same method applies; what changes is the media representatives asked to attend.

Usually the invitation to a news conference is extended by phone. This procedure serves two purposes. It establishes a sense of immediacy, and it enables the caller to ask for a commitment—will the medium be on hand or won't it? Too aggressive an approach can turn off a potential attendee; too timid an approach can cause an editor to decide the event lacks importance.

On the business level, one should not assume that the importance he attaches to his news event is contagious. He should, therefore, be prepared to justify the reason for the news conference to those he calls, but he must not lapse into an argument, an apology, or a sales pitch. If an editor says, "I just don't think that's important enough to send someone," there are only two answers: (1) "I really hope you do send someone because the story really is important and can't just be covered in a news release," or (2) "I'll send you a news release on this so that you'll have the story."

The more important the conference, the less important it is to play host, but if there's any chance the conference might not start on time, have refreshments for those who arrive early. This step can prevent the problems that occur when it's time for the conference to start and some of the expected reporters haven't arrived.

If television crews are expected, provide a "line drop" if possible. This is nothing more than a 25-amp, 120-volt outlet into which the crew can plug its lights. Using wall outlets means this risk: A circuit breaker can blow in the middle of a speech or commentary, and without lights there will be no usable film.

It's time for your conference to begin. Here are twelve rules to give the conference a professional patina:

1. Start within ten minutes of the announced time.
2. Don't make long, flowery speeches.
3. Have press kits on hand to distribute to all media representatives, with extras for those who don't attend but might run a story.
4. Have adequate seats but not too many. Have a stack of extra folding chairs in an adjoining room.
5. Have something visual on hand—large photographic blowups, model units, charts or maps, or a display.

6. If the press kit contains a specific announcement, repeat it; then from careful notes ad-lib additional commentary.

7. Have extra people on hand in case attendance is thin.

8. Avoid mugging the cameras, either still or motion picture.

9. Allow questions and answer them candidly.

10. Have at least one person primed to ask the first question if none comes spontaneously.

11. Anticipate a total length of twenty to thirty minutes.

12. Don't wait for a "Thank you, Mr. President." When the questions have petered out, thank those present and invite them to stay for refreshments. Stay yourself to answer any further questions that might be asked by those not in a hurry to leave.

Like all potent weapons, a news conference can be dynamite, but improperly planned and handled, it can explode in your face.

Research

Sharing the information that stems from an analysis of research is excellent public relations, not only because it suggests both scholarship and dedication to the subject, but also because the information often is useful to the public to whom the information is funneled.

Media usually are willing to print or repeat excerpts of research significant to their readership or audience. Even some research that is blatantly commercial in nature nonetheless receives wide dissemination for no reason other than the fact that it *is* research.

You may feel that only educational institutions and research-oriented associations are capable of research that has public relations overtones. While these are the primary sources of large-scale research projects, the world of commerce spawns much research worthy of news coverage, and much more would be done were the typical businessman aware of how beneficial research might be, not only for the information it gives him but also for the image it can build.

Suppose, for example, that you are in the insurance business. You decide to mount, by mail or phone, a primitive research project: Is the average individual in your community carrying more or less insurance than he did a year ago? Five hundred people, unrelated to your own client list, are polled, and the tabulated results show that the average person carries 10 percent more automobile insurance and 15 percent less homeowners' insurance.

The business use you might make of this information is unrelated to this book, but the public relations value is substantial. Consider a news release that begins:

> Residents of Jonestown are spending more for car insurance, but less for homeowners' insurance, than they did a year ago.
>
> A recently completed citywide survey of 500 homeowners and renters by the Smith Insurance Agency showed a 10 percent increase in auto protection and a 15 percent decrease in homeowners' coverage.
>
> According to John J. Smith, who sponsored the study, "One obvious reason might be the statewide increase in the cost of current model autos, but another reason might be. . . .

What's the value? Smith is established as an authority. His agency has shown itself to be interested not just in selling insurance, but also in analysis. Smith can use the results in mailings to clients and prospective clients; and he becomes, through this one activity, someone to be interviewed, to make a speech, and to become a spokesman for his particular kind of business.

Some businessmen fear research because they have been trained to feel that it is a highly specialized and highly expensive art, unapproachable except by experts who mutter an esoteric jargon and punch strange codes into computers. It's true that what might be considered "major" research uses equipment, techniques, and specialists with a background no businessman could begin to approach, but research designed to obtain facts for interpretation (rather than facts with interpretation implicit in the information), and research that does not attempt to get answers indirectly by a "psychological" approach, can be handled by anyone with a logical mind and an understanding of how to tabulate the results.

This point is clarified by comparing public relations research with so-called "pure" research. For example, a political candidate easily can discover his current position through a single question: "If the election were held today, would you vote for Mr. A, Mr. B, or Mr. C?" If the sample were at all representative, he would have useful information.

But if the candidate wanted to cross-check his *image* against other candidates, or if he wanted to learn areas of political weakness or strength in the minds of voters, he might well have to hire a professional research organization.

Be sure, in conducting a research project, that the people you "sample" are representative of the group that should be sampled. If you're learning about attitudes of the residents of Johnstown, questions should be asked of the residents of Johnstown, not of outsiders. And beware of the danger of getting a mass sample, in one place, that will destroy the validity of the results. For example, a group of children in a playground, a group of women at a concert, a group of businesspeople at a merchants' meeting, or a group of churchgoers on a Sunday morning should be sampled sparingly (unless they represent the single group you want).

Educational institutions are among the greatest generators of research, for two valid reasons:

1.   Research is involved in many courses and in the pursuit of advanced degrees; thus, at some schools faculty and students aggressively seek out subjects on which to do research.

2.   For projects that require "legmen," physical subjects

for experimentation, or the prestige necessary to elicit responses from a high percentage of subjects approached, the student/faculty situation is uniquely convenient.

If this is true, why doesn't more research sponsored by various departments of schools and colleges surface in print? Much research is lost only because of pedants who guard results jealously and refuse to indulge even their own public relations departments by turning over a copy of the results. Much is lost because those actually doing the research are unaware of the prestige and benefits that can accrue *outside* the technical area in which the research is done. And much is lost because tabulations are made not to inform outsiders but to educate insiders. Thus the student who spends an entire semester researching magazine readership habits or industrial resistance to metric conversions hands in his paper, gets his grade, and sees his information disappear into the educational maw.

One of the most successful public relations oriented research projects a college can mount is also one of the easiest —a follow-up study of its own graduates, tracing their jobs and incomes.

The businessman can limit himself to simple, easy-to-organize research and still end up with information of great use to the people he wants to influence. A real estate broker has a bright assistant call (or interview) local lending institutions. He then assembles the information into an analysis of the local money market.

One need not look for deadly serious subject matter in order to achieve success in commercially aimed research. A project described with a sense of humor might well gain as much press attention as an expensive poll summarized in academic jargon.

A hotel circularizes its clientele, or simply searches its own files, seeking information. Serious subjects for research might include questions such as these: Where do guests come from? How long do they stay? But the hotel might also reach print with questions such as these: What initial is most common among its guests' last names? What kind of egg is most preferred in the coffee shop? What's the average number of pieces of luggage? Even though some of this information is not particularly enlightening, it makes interesting copy.

The serious department store might analyze buying patterns over the year; and, assuming the store's competitors didn't do the same, the results might be well received by media. But that same store can keep its name in print and maintain a sophisticated image by revealing the most popular color of shirts bought in its menswear section; the ratio of tennis equipment sold in comparison with football, baseball, softball, or fishing gear; and the most popular size frying pan sold in its housewares department.

Obviously, any such publicized research should be information beneficial to the store. There is *no* point publicizing information which might damage the store's competitive position.

Such businesses as employment agencies, associations and societies, sports teams, and travel agents have an easy time of it, because the seeds of interesting information from research are right there in what they do. With less public-oriented businesses, the possibilities might not be so obvious; but this author states flatly: There is *no* business that cannot find within its own structure a means of using research, not only for personal information, but also for public relations success.

Community Participation

When a community celebrates a holiday, has street parades, has a school homecoming, starts amateur sports leagues, or approaches standard events such as elections or memorial days, many businessmen groan at the thought of participating. They regard such events as albatrosses around their necks when they should welcome the opportunity to use these activities as touchstones for their own public relations programs. Legitimacy is superimposed on everything they do to participate in such a publicly acceptable event.

Consider street parades. A businessman can give an award to the best float, the best band, the best costume, or the parade queen; he can enter a float of his own; he can sponsor the appearance of a high school band from another area; he can enter the parade in an antique car; he can give lemonade to all the marchers. Any of these moves will bring him not only publicity but goodwill.

If the parade is a Thanksgiving or Christmas parade, the businessman should look for a means of tying his participation not only into the event but also into his own type of business without appearing objectionably commercial. Thus a dairy might have an inflated balloon cow; a lumberyard might have an inflated Paul Bunyan; a bakery might have a huge (billed as "the world's largest") inflated loaf of bread.

Such participation should not be considered only by retailers. Merchants tend to dominate such affairs, but they do so only because other businessmen don't think of the public relations benefits they can realize from involvement.

Nonprofit organizations have the easiest time of it in community participations. Not only do they enjoy exemption from the normal rules of nonpushy behavior, but they are in the singular position of organizing the entire community into a single promotional unit. The community chest, the chamber of commerce, a local hospital, the high school or a local college, an association of religious organizations— these, provided they can avoid both wild-eyed enthusiasm for unproducible ideas and cold-blooded professionalism with no apparent enthusiasm at all, can organize businessmen and media together into a coherent whole, in which the businessman who normally would never cooperate in such a promotion will grow a beard (because others are growing beards), donate use of a key display window for a month (because others are donating theirs), and give money (because position in the community cannot be jeopardized).

Two typical examples of a community-wide project might be a centennial celebration and a day or week of nonsectarian prayer. Sponsors of the first are usually the town's commercial establishments, and sponsors of the second are the town's religious or scholastic leaders. Both would, through a carefully compiled list of activities (each of which would have its own chairman and committee), offer involvement in at least one activity to every adult and child living or working in the community.

A centennial might include these activities:

1. A kickoff parade involves local musical and marching groups, similar groups from other areas, business-sponsored floats, and every major business, fraternal, civic, labor, religious, and social organization.

2. A short subject is prepared for motion picture theatres, produced in 35mm color and printed in 35mm for theatrical viewing and 16mm for television and other distribution. The film traces the history of the area. Its cost is underwritten by public subscription—a goal of one dollar per resident for communities of fifteen to twenty-five thousand people is ample. Or perhaps a single major industry located in the town will pay the entire cost.

3. Retail windows hold historical displays for a month. In proper sequence, the windows tell the history of the area. Each retailer works with a group—a school class or members of a club. A directory will credit every participant and allow visitors to study windows in proper sequence.

4. During Centennial Month, adult men wear beards; adult women wear costumes whenever possible; and children iron centennial decals onto T-shirts. Bumper stickers and road signs are reminders for visitors as well as residents.

5. For Centennial Month, the main street becomes a

mall with kiddie rides, amusements, and sidewalk specials. Steam locomotives take the populace for nostalgic rides, and horse-drawn carts carry winners of free rides through the park or along a historic trail.

6. In some windows, members of the Boy Scouts or Girl Scouts appear during the day, churning butter, hammering horseshoes, operating looms and spinning wheels, or making old-fashioned candy and bread (for sale).

While this example uses a centennial as the touchstone, a bicentennial, a diamond anniversary, or a "salute" (to the Space Age, to a local event that has historical merit, to the hundredth birthday of a local leader, to the establishment of the first school, college, church, business, library, or railroad station) all are valid bases for this type of promotion, provided the leadership comes from an impeccable civic source and is endorsed by proper political and business leaders.

Even more challenging to the imagination is the salute to something that has no specific local tie. It is, however, the kind of community promotion that can bring in network television crews and wire service reporters. If it becomes an annual event, it can in time become regional and national, with your community as the hub of activities.

Our example will be called World Hope Week. It is based on the conclusion by the religious leaders of the community, in concert with educators and those politicians whose names are not linked with partisan politics, that the international situation is serious, that there is much ethnic misunderstanding, that brotherhood among nations is not an impossible dream, and that this one community will attempt, on its own, to sponsor and foster events that will show that one community has hope for the future.

World Hope Week might include these activities:

1. Scheduled music and dancing in the public square. Each hour a different ethnic or national group would perform. As many countries as possible would be represented, in cos-

tume and in song. Publicity about the event might well bring groups from other areas, so participation by ethnic groups that might well be at hand (such as persons from England, Mexico, Germany, Poland, and Italy) are reinforced by groups that might be available from neighboring communities (such as persons from India, countries of Africa, Japan, Russia, the Philippines, France, Czechoslovakia, or Greece). It is conceivable that an album of music can be cut, featuring the groups as they appear. The album would be used as a gift and premium as well as for sale through local stores.

2. A street parade featuring all the groups, plus as many invited participants as you can find. The parade can be in the evening or, if the city is cooperative, on a business day, down the main street. An appointed committee awards prizes for the best costumes, most inventive ideas, best floats, best ethnic music, longest distance traveled, best business participation, best club participation, and best school participation.

3. Dedication of store windows to the theme. The concept can spread to office lobbies and industrial fronts.

4. A heavy program of media participation. Spokesmen should arrange for interviews throughout the preparatory period and during the event itself. Press materials should be available well in advance, with photographs and a daily schedule of news releases. Television stations should be apprised of the timing of especially visual activities, and a line drop should be provided for interiors or night activities requiring lighting. Public service slides, film, recordings, and print ads should be delivered to each medium with the request that they be aired or printed during the event.

5. A World Hope Week logo, individualistic and highly visible. The logo should be available in the form of decals, heat-transfers (for T-shirts), etch proofs (for letterheads and mailings), and buttons and bumper stickers sold on a self-liquidating basis (that is, with income from sale covering the

costs) to those who will wear or display them. A banner, to hang above the main street, also should bear the emblem.

6. Participation by consulates. Most recognized foreign governments have consulates in major cities besides their main embassies in Washington. Representatives can be invited to participate in the parade and to give speeches.

7. A final street banquet. This is the climax of World Hope Week, and booths, tables, and tents will hold foods of all nations. For one fee, which includes a donation to help underwrite the event, diners eat all they want of foods prepared by the many organizations that are participating— foods representing every country, including America.

One might ask, "What is the meaning of all this? Why bother? What purpose is served?"

Altruism is hard to explain; so is dedication. But for purposes of study and adaptation, think rather in terms of a community problem affecting the area in which you live or in which your company is located. Might not a selfless special event, dedicated to brotherhood or peace, do much to instill community spirit—and put the town on network television while it does so?

Other Civic Gestures

A businessman has other ways in which he can show his interest in the community and achieve positive public relations while he does so. He can associate with civic clubs such as Rotary, Kiwanis, Friends of the Library, the Variety Club. On occasion he can cooperate with a fund-raising venture and make promotional capital from it. For example, a restaurant can match dollars with a club holding a fund-raising dinner on its premises. A developer can make available an empty store as a "haunted house" for Halloween in which the club mounts witch, goblin, and skeleton displays and fright shows to raise funds. Any businessman can arrange to hire students on a work-study program or to show how his business works to appropriate groups of high school or college students.

A businessman can sponsor teams—softball teams, bowling teams, even bridge teams. As the teams compete, the very nature of local news reporting brings the name into print.

A businessman can participate in (or, if he has the time and abilities, *organize*) pro-am sports events in which players pay for the privilege of playing with the pros and, in doing so, contribute to the charity named as the beneficiary.

A businessman also can donate his own time to the chamber of commerce, the parent-teacher association, or any number of worthy local groups anxious to have him as a participant. As his own worth to the organization increases, his responsibilities and the resulting press attention increase.

Stunts

A model dives into the river; she wears a new wrinkle-free raincoat sold at a local store.

A policeman is invited to shoot a hole in a new self-sealing tire mounted on the car of the local dealer who then will drive on it to show that it is intact.

Twenty youngsters hula-hoop themselves to exhaustion in a marathon in a prominent display window of a department store.

Stunts, which usually indicate a sense of humor as well as a flair for the theatrical, often bring heavy coverage. They also can backfire by giving the sponsor of the stunt the image of a nincompoop.

There is nothing wrong with a stunt, provided that it is not so ridiculous, so stupid, or so trite that stunt-wise media will not cover it (or, worse, will cover it with wisecracks and derogation).

Use of pretty girls, children, and dogs generally means

safety for the stunt. Use of noise, paint, and mess usually means danger.

Showing the strength of a lawn-mower motor by having a girl ride the mower a hundred miles is a salesworthy stunt because the stunt relates to the product being promoted. Being hit in the face with a whipped-cream pie is an obvious cry for attention with no thoughtfulness—unless you're a pie manufacturer advertising a "throwing model."

Unless it's an unusually heavy news day, media tend to show up to cover stunts. Sometimes you send them only a teaser—"Something unusual will happen at the corner of Fourth and State at 11 A.M. Bring your cameras." Sometimes your description is more specific: "A hundred years of grime will be washed off a hundred bricks on the old building at Fourth and State, between 11 and 11:30 A.M."

If there is one rule for stunts, it is *rehearse first.* A quiet tryout will avoid the embarrassment that becomes a public joke when the stunt doesn't come off.

Stunts, properly executed, can result in strong press coverage. Many are suggested in Chapter 10.

7

internal public relations

Who is the public with whom you want to establish and maintain relations? When you ask yourself that question, you can gain much by looking inside as well as outside. Whenever an organization grows larger than two people, someone is bound to say, "I don't know" to an outsider every day.

Internal public relations is largely a matter of maintaining *communication* with those in your organization. Some who fail to understand the subtleties of internal public relations regard such activities as hopeless: "My employees don't give a damn," they say; or, "No matter what we tell them, only the same handful ever does anything"; or, "Why bother? The union tells them to ignore anything they hear from us."

Remember that understanding and agreement stem from communication; with it, you still may not accomplish any goals of internal public relations; without it, you *surely* won't.

House Organs

A house organ is a publication by and for an in-group. It is the most common method of internal public relations:

—A fast food chain will distribute a monthly newsletter to its franchise operators. The newsletter not only describes changes in business structure; it also has folksy, newsy items that enable the publisher to include as many names of operators as possible.

—A college publishes an alumni newspaper. The newspaper devotes some space to faculty, buildings, and honors; but it always includes news of alumni, and this portion is best read.

—A department store mimeographs a daily bulletin to its employees. It not only tells what changes have been made in administration and management; it also describes the day's specials, changes in hours, changes in department locations, and other information that the employees in turn can transmit to a customer who asks.

—An ethical pharmaceuticals manufacturer publishes a slick magazine. Printed in full color on enamel paper, with a heavy cover, the publication rivals in both production and content the best of the trade magazines. In addition to its employees, the manufacturer distributes copies to shareholders, to media, to prospective customers, to medical schools and doctors, and to people whose opinions can build image.

—An association sends a monthly bulletin to its members. By glorifying the participation of the truly active members, the association hopes to spur others to action. And members are constantly reminded that this is an alive, busy organization in which they should renew their membership.

All these are examples of house organs. By definition a house organ is intramural: it is designed to circulate to a *vertical interest group.* Too many house-organ publishers make the mistakes of underestimating the size of the group and failing to include those with peripheral involvement.

Typically, a house organ will have departments such as these:

1. News of the organization—what has happened since the last issue was published.

2. News of people—what they have accomplished relative to the existence and continuation of the organization, including honors and awards.

3. Personals—births, marriages, sports activities.

4. Photographs (assuming that the printing method permits reproduction) of activities, equipment, conventions, people on the job, new executives.

5. Contributed articles by members of the group.

6. Management's point of view—the logical rationale for publication of many house organs.

Because management tends toward overkill, watch for too much "viewpoint" when inserting that sixth component. Hard-core editorializing may well alienate those whom you're trying to influence.

House organs usually have a magazine format, but many are laid out as tabloid newspapers and others are issued as newsletters. The format depends not only on the amount of information to be included but also on the budget and the image the house organ is expected to project.

Cold-type composing machines and low-cost instant printers have helped phase out the old-fashioned mimeographed or dittoed house organs. There no longer exists a strong rationale for using a typewriter as finished format, the single exception being a newsletter that attempts to convey an appearance of urgency. Some house organs, therefore, include one page of typed "hot news." Invariably, this section is the most read because it appears to be most urgent.

One easy way to achieve a two-color well-produced look is to *prerun* in quantity the logo or nameplate in a color other than black. If your house organ plans a circulation of 500 per issue, run 3,000. Then, in groups of 500, run each month's issue in black. The colored banner will contrast with the standard black and improve the appearance of the product. Cost? Very little, since you've gang-run the portion that doesn't change.

Because production of a house organ always starts out as great fun and shortly becomes a terrible chore, the publisher of a house organ can ease his job and make friends at the same time—Tom Sawyer and the fence—by appointing subeditors. There can be a general news editor, a sports editor, a personals editor, a photography editor, and perhaps a feature editor. Each will have regularly allocated space and each will have the responsibility for supplying—subject to reasonable editorial controls—written material to fill that space. Mention in the masthead makes each editor a celebrity (itself a good move in internal public relations) and increases dedication.

The key to success of a house organ is relevance to the reader. Allowing an internal publication to degenerate into a dull reflection of an in-group is an excellent way to kill off readership and interest.

House organs that circulate among employees of a company should maximize use of those employees. They should not be simply "mouthpieces" of the management, and house organs that achieve high readership and therefore high impact follow this relatively simple rule. In an area in which the dividing line between labor and management is ever psychologically widening, a communication as simple and controllable as a house organ is both logical and obvious.

Those house organs which circulate to members of an organization obviously should exploit the benefits of membership; they also should publicize the activities of members who have achieved worthwhile goals on behalf of the organization. But one problem that arises more than it should is that such publications become the instruments of an in-group, in which the same people appear over and over again—with everyone else looked upon as outsiders. This is an editorial challenge which behooves the individual responsible for editorial content to avoid seeking out those same sources issue after issue.

The writer of a house organ circulating to customers of a business firm might well remember that they *are* customers and that use of the pages for self-aggrandizement must be limited. Often, an industrial company sending its house organ to its customers overlooks the customers' interests and uses the house organ simply as a "puff."

If ads are to be included in such a publication, let them be a "hotlist" of specials for preferred customers, properly labeled and forthrightly presented as what they are—products for sale.

Memos and Recordings

The use of memos as a public relations tool should not be overlooked, since memos are the lowest-cost, most urgent-appearing means of communication.

Too many businessmen use memos only on the one-to-one level, to transmit information, demands, or questions in anticipation of a one-to-one response. An analysis of the structure of the memo shows that this apparently primitive means of communication can be valuable. Receipt of a memo is personal. It is implicitly not a mass communication and is, therefore, selective. Thus, sending a group of memos, even if all are identical, suggests selecting a special group of individuals and treating them as individuals, regardless of the message.

Many who would not respond to any other appeal, even a telephone conversation, will respond to a memo because of the status it implies. Memos are a logical psychological tool for management to use when presenting viewpoint.

Lightweight plastic recordings, which can be included in a five-by-seven envelope, have become a popular means for transmission of not just a message, but the message in the voice of the person transmitting that message. But since "decoding" equipment is needed, consider the limitations along with the advantages. Too many of these recordings are put on a table, on a desk, or worse, in a drawer: "I'll play it when I have my phonograph at hand." That "when" never arrives.

There is, incidentally, a certain pomposity to recordings, and unless the recipient is tuned to the sender, it can be less effective than many other means of communication.

Cassette recordings are a popular means of personalized communication in the late 1970s. But such communication is best used as a one-to-one means of transmitting information. The mass dissemination of information by cassettes is not only costly, but it may be less effective than printed communication on such a level. The advantage of the cassette is its personal impact: it represents a communication from one person to another and it is in the ability to underscore and emphasize by voice that cassettes are most effective.

Meetings and Conventions

The advantage of meetings or conventions in public relations is that the sponsor can, for an average of three days, literally hold captive the people with whom he wants to have forced communication. (Forced communication is the method of transmitting controlled information with two anticipated results: 1) absorption and appreciation of the information; 2) a positive and desired action taken as the result of the communication.)

Years ago, a group of engineers, salesmen, or dealers would gather for three days of speeches in a Chicago or Miami hotel. They were expected to attend most of the sessions—usually a breakfast session beginning about 8:30 in the morning and ending at 10:00, a later morning session beginning at 10:00 and ending at noon, a luncheon session from noon to 2:00, and one or two afternoon sessions—for each of three days. There might also be a "president's banquet" or a "dress-up" dinner to close the sessions.

While many conventions still use this traditional form,

other developments have made possible the expansion of this kind of public relations activity far beyond its original concept. One such development is the charter airplane, which, with low fares for "affinity groups," has made possible meetings in exotic cities from Istanbul to Melbourne. Why meet in Istanbul or Melbourne? One reason is that the sponsor of a meeting or convention to some extent lives in terror not only of boring his audience but also of having them mutter when next year's meeting site is announced, "Aw, nuts! We've been there twice before!" Thus meetings are now held on boats traveling from Miami to the Bahamas; on trains churning through the Transylvanian Alps; and even in the lounge of a 747 jet, as a kickoff session for a convention that might begin even before the plane touches down at its destination. Meeting sponsors have begun to look not only for different locations; some seek the bizarre. And the meeting itself becomes secondary to the meeting site.

This new look in meetings and conventions has spawned a whole new industry. The meeting and convention specialists will not only plan the meetings themselves, being certain that the electrical connections in the hotel meeting room at Bangkok match the plugs on the projectors, but will involve themselves in side trips to scenic places, in the travel arrangements, and in the construction of display units and exhibits that become an integral part of the meeting. (It should be made clear that the international meeting, with its problems in logistics, passports, decisions on points of departure, and occasional tax disallowances, should not be considered the standard way of life as yet. But the growth of this arm of business meetings has been spectacular.)

The small businessperson or the unknown member of a large organization may feel outclassed or outmanned in the milieu of a large meeting. Take heart: not only are there many levels of meetings, but also the little guy benefits constantly by the apathy of many of the big guys.

Rather than discard the suggestions for public relations

opportunities at meetings and conventions because "I'm too small," think in terms of what you can do and how you can do it to become part of the in-group whose names (and therefore public relations value) are well-known because they invariably organize, control, and speak for an organization. It is logical to believe that your help will be welcome, and in serving your own public relations goals you serve those of the organization as well.

What is the public relations value of a meeting or a convention? To examine the benefits, the problems, and the means of exploiting them to their fullest potential, meetings and conventions should be separated. Technically, a convention is more public relations-oriented than is a meeting. This is because normally a meeting represents a group whose income is controlled by the person holding the meeting; a convention is a group with a common interest—either a group of professionals meeting once or twice a year to exchange ideas or a group of dealers whose income does not depend entirely on one manufacturer or distributor.

For a meeting, distinct parameters must be set up delineating who is to be included, what subjects will be discussed, and why. If the meeting is a sales meeting (by far the most common formal type of meeting) then the question arises: which salesmen will be invited and is there a qualification to attend?

For example, a major company with two hundred men on the road may decide to have a sales meeting in Hawaii. Since the meeting implicitly is 50 percent vacation, the company may provide an incentive in a bulletin to its salesmen: "You will qualify to attend this meeting at our expense if you sell a minimum of $50,000 worth of merchandise during the next six-month period." This gives an immediate goal to salesmen and creates a reward for performance.

Obviously the company is not entirely altruistic. A properly run sales meeting should result in dramatically improved sales for the period immediately following the meeting. If it doesn't, you might well ask whether the meeting itself has been properly motivated, organized, and effected. Simply to have a meeting with no commercial goal is to waste the dollars spent on the meeting in the first place. Any meeting, whether sales-oriented or not, should have as its underlying theme a statement of purpose by the individuals responsible for the organization of that meeting. Why are we here? What do we anticipate as the result?

Some meetings are sponsored by one company to introduce new products or to kick off promotional campaigns. In such cases, the meeting sessions must be carefully structured so that those who attend understand clearly by the time they leave the meeting site exactly what is expected of them and what actions they are to take. They must grasp all the information that makes possible their participation in the organized kickoff of the campaign.

What to Do and What to Say. Many people who sponsor meetings, even locally, tend to pussyfoot because of fear that they are commandeering too much of the time of the people attending. On the local level, an insurance executive might say to himself, "I've forced all these men to attend this dinner. I don't want them to hate me for spending the evening lecturing them."

Such fears are more than foolish. They overlook the reason for the meeting in the first place. If one wants to entertain, he need not have a meeting at all; he can mail tickets or hire comedians. The purpose of the meeting is to transmit information, and seeing to it that people have a good time is excellent psychology but is in no way a substitute for the meeting itself. The key to successful meetings is to strike the proper balance between an attempt to organize every minute of what becomes an overstructured work session and a "cruise-director" approach that is so pleasure-oriented that the purpose of the meeting becomes murky and its goals lost through overattention to sightseeing, shopping, and shows.

Meetings that the average businessman is asked to attend will not be this exotic or this long. He may have a call from a distributor of goods who will say to him, "Joe, can you join us for breakfast next Tuesday from 7:30 until 9:30? One of the big guns from our company will be in town and we asked some of our dealers to join us at the Sheraton Hotel so that we can show you some changes in merchandising that might make a buck for you." The entire session, then, lasts two hours. Under such circumstances it is mandatory that the sponsor of the meeting end it on time, because goodwill is quickly dissipated when those attending begin to look at their watches after the meeting has run twenty minutes late and shows no sign of terminating.

Within a company, an employee will be asked to attend a meeting of the entire staff or of his particular section. This meeting will be mandatory, since the sponsor controls the economic destiny of those invited. But, just as it is a mistake to be too pleasure-oriented, it also is a mistake to be so coldly businesslike that the meeting deteriorates into a harangue or a note-taking session that demoralizes those attending.

Typically the speakers at business meetings are not professional speakers, and professional coaching can make an enormous difference not only in the impact of the speech but also in its public relations value. The coach, however, should work within the speaker's style. A few years ago the president of the United States hired a joke writer as one of his speech writers, to the chagrin of his associates and of the White House reporters. The method was ineffective because a speech suddenly, with no regard for logic, would have a joke dropped like a broken egg into its middle. It was apparent to anyone listening that the joke was not genuine or in context.

Today, semiprofessional speechmakers often rehearse

their speeches on videotape. They then replay them for their associates and deliberately subject themselves to criticism, no matter how brutal, in an attempt to have that speech be as effective as possible. But too many overlook the reality that they may be able to address the group only once a year, and the image they transmit is the image that these people will carry away with them. What image will the listeners perceive? An image of stodginess? Of stupidity? Of silliness? Of emotion? Of coldness?

Not all people are the same and not all speeches should be the same, but the nonprofessional speaker should take every precaution to assure himself that not only the content but the delivery of his speech matches the mood, the circumstances, and the ultimate impression he wants to convey to his target audience.

How Conventions Differ.   A convention represents a more sociable activity than a meeting since those who attend are usually not economically dependent on the organization or sponsor hosting the convention. However, danger lies in waltzing casually into unstructured sessions and paying too little attention to the business reasons for holding the convention. When the time comes for next year's convention, attendance might suffer because of what happened this year.

Conventions normally have five components: (1) the business sessions, (2) the exhibits, (3) the interplay, (4) the social events, and (5) the side trips and auxiliary travel.

The interplay among people attending the convention is the most important part from the viewpoint of getting individuals to attend. Often, conventioneers do not see each other between conventions, and they look forward not to the business sessions but to the opportunity of seeing their friends. Therefore, one should not schedule so many sessions, or schedule sessions so close together, that socializing is difficult. The result of tight scheduling is that socializing decreases attendance at the sessions, which is self-defeating in convention planning.

If the convention invites outside exhibitors and charges them a fee for the right to show their wares, exhibit hours must be ample. A sound philosophy might be the more the better. The reason is that an exhibitor often counts the number of people visiting his booth. He doesn't count wives and friends separately; each person is a unit. His decision to exhibit again next year will be affected by the total number of people he has seen. It might be logical to limit attendance at business sessions to dues-paying members but to open the exhibition sessions to anyone interested.

When selecting the site, the planner of a meeting or a convention must consider factors ranging from hotel rates to geographical location. Some magnificent resorts, located in areas that are a two-hour drive from the nearest airport, might be unsuitable if proper transportation cannot be arranged. On the other hand, these isolated resorts often advertise themselves as good meeting sites because there, unlike major metropolitan centers, those in attendance do not readily slip away, missing sessions in favor of the night life or scenic wonders of the city.

Large conventions often are planned two to five years in advance to assure the group an ample number of hotel rooms and the proper facilities. The first-time planner should read the trade magazines in the meetings and convention field and familiarize himself with the terminology and with the multiplicity of decisions he must make to avoid the embarrassment of an important oversight that can destroy the effectiveness of his sessions. For example:

Are all meeting rooms free of charge?

Can you demand a projectionist, an electrician, a public address system, or desks? What are the charges for each?

Will the hotel supply a limousine for pickup and delivery of guests at the airport?

Can you obtain a free executive suite for the president of the organization?

If the convention is booked several years ahead, what protection does either party have as to rate changes?

Standard agreements exist, and using them will assure at least a minimum of professionalism in planning.

Starting with Your Own Personnel

Image-building outside the organization is flatly impossible without the cooperation of your employees who have contact with the public. Whatever you say about yourself can be given the lie through employee thoughtlessness, carelessness, or indolence.

Imagine the mood of a theatregoer who gets the "New York City treatment" from a box-office clerk. If the patron dares to ask a single question or suggests that his seats are not the best, the resulting outburst will assure that he will enter the auditorium in the most poisonous of moods, cursing the theatre rather than the ticket-seller since he regards the ticket-seller as spokesman for the house. (A relatively famous story concerns the surliness, curtness, and short tempers of some ticket-sellers. Asked whether he couldn't teach his box-office people to be polite, the manager answered, "Oh, no. They're unionized.")

Retail clerks similarly are in a powerful position to make or break image with a store's customers. The customer probably never meets the owner of the store, nor even the managers of departments. Thus, instructions to new personnel should include more information than how to punch a time clock and where the washrooms are. The approach should be: "Other stores may not care what customers think of them. We do. And our slogan is 'Be polite if it kills you.' No, the customer isn't always right. But our employee who loses his temper is always wrong."

Industrial workers often feel that their loyalty is to the union, not to the individual who makes their jobs possible. This attitude cannot be overcome by rhetoric. But one can hope to temper any apathy toward the company by imparting a sense of pride. Athletic teams, company events, and house organs do more than coffee breaks, because the former are not quickly taken for granted.

Instilling a sense of pride is no one-shot matter. It is a continuing educational job that results in such obvious benefits as a bright voice answering your phone, a neat uniform on an attendant or worker, the absence of obscenities scratched in the washroom stalls, an overall pleasant atmosphere, and reduced employee turnover.

The leading bowler on your team is not about to quit his job with your company; the girl who was featured as Miss Personality in your house organ will try to justify the title; and the employee who has won a plaque for an innovation or for meritorious service will be your booster, not your detractor.

Some businessmen feel that any organization with less than fifty employees is too small for intramural public relations. But the wise small employer knows that while an internal house organ might be foolish for ten employees, it isn't foolish to feature one of them each month in a mailing to clients or customers. He knows that once a week he should lunch with several of his staff (not with just one, which starts rumors flying). And he knows that while democracy seldom works in business, he can at least listen to suggestions of any nature whatever without compromising his own stature.

Employee attitude can be the cause of many dollars made or lost by the company. The cost of intramural public relations almost always is less than the cost of personnel problems such actions can prevent.

How Your Phone Is Answered

The way your phone is answered says a lot about the image you are projecting *and* about the success of your internal public relations program. A memorable test is to leave your office and make ten phone calls: nine to other offices and one to your own.

You'll find that some people make you feel important from the moment they answer the phone. If the employee is well trained, he or she will be pleasant, polite, and, most important of all, apparently unhurried. Your call seems important.

At other places you're treated to surliness, apathy, and a casual evaluation of the importance of your business, and you tend to dislike the organization even before you reach the person you're calling.

Since the first impression is the hardest one to erase, consider imposing these phone-answering rules in your own office:

1. If a caller must be put on "hold," allow no more than thirty seconds to elapse before cutting back into the call to determine whether that caller wants to stay on hold, wants to call back, or wants to be called back.

2. If someone asks, "Is Mr. Jones in?" answer yes or no before asking who's calling. To ask who's calling *before* answering the question implies that Jones is in to some and out to others.

3. Each employee (even you) should place his or her own calls. Nothing infuriates a busy person more than to pick up the receiver and be told, "One moment please for Mr. Smith," and then to hang on the dead phone while Smith takes his own good time picking up his phone to complete a call he himself originated.

4. If you take a call when you are genuinely too busy to talk, apologize and ask, "May I call you back?" instead

of giving the impression that you're too busy to bother with the caller.

5. If you are in a meeting and are having your calls held, the person answering the phone should explain this at once to the person calling. Don't suddenly decide you're not taking calls after the caller has already been given the impression that you're available.

6. If you have several phone lines, one rule should be absolute: When only one line is available, no one should make an outgoing call. Invariably, the person who calls and gets a busy signal is the one who has just decided to do business with you and whose attitude is too fragile to damage.

Some businessmen never see their clients or customers; they meet and deal with them only by phone. Telephone procedure can be an important public relations plus—or minus.

8 eleemosynary public relations

Don't let the title of this chapter scare you. *Eleemosynary* (pronounced el-uh-mo-suh-nar-ee) simply means devoted to charitable purposes.

Fund-raising in today's complicated and multi-faceted society is a business for professionals. And professional fund-raisers are highly trained and highly paid.

Not all charities can afford the high-powered pro, but they can use the same techniques he uses and enjoy what, in the eleemosynary world, is the ultimate, the pinnacle: causing people to contribute not only without hating you for having pushed them, but actually loving you because their donations were swapped either for a good time or for personal publicity.

Using the Mails

Some of the eleemosynary rules are mechanical, and the first of these is to spend the money to send mail first class. Consistent users of the mails report that invariably a solicitation sent first class will outdraw one sent third class, far in excess of the cost differential.

Another rule is to put stamps on your return reply envelopes. Ordinarily a mailer will use business reply envelopes so that he pays postage only for those pieces of mail actually returned. In fund-raising, however, pasting a real first-class stamp on the reply envelope, while obviously creating some waste, often increases the response enormously. Why? One of the big keys to fund-raising is *guilt*. The sender has already bought a stamp. We owe him something.

In the prehistoric days of the 1960s, fund-raisers packed their mailings with tears and sadness—dependable instruments for drawing dollars from donors. But in the Age of Skepticism, tears and sadness are so commonplace, so overused, and so lacking in impact that to compete in the eleemosynary marketplace they must be combined with those two great motivators of the last quarter of the twentieth century—greed and guilt.

Fear is still a potent motivator, but fear is generally unacceptable as a long-range technique, since supporters after a time tend to drift away to a less demanding charity.

The pull of mailings tends to go up when the individual piece of mail is signed not by the head of the institution or by a civic personality, but by an individual personally known to the recipient. A political structure has been superimposed on many fund-raising drives. A steering committee is formed to recruit additional workers. Each member of the committee leans on friends, relatives, and business underlings, who form his own committee. It is this group who sign the letters to the public; each subcommittee member may have the responsibility of signing a hundred letters or providing a hundred names to receive letters to which his name will be appended.

Public Relations and Fund-Raising

News editors come to feel that a new reason to raise funds is started every day. There is fierce competition for publicity, made worse by amateurs who demand media coverage without offering even the most primitive reason or help as an excuse: "You gave a lot of space to the United Fund and the college. We need coverage too." The news or features editors are left to invent the story rationale; instead, they are likely to ignore the whole thing.

Dilettantes and amateurs make up the public relations "committees" of many fund-raising organizations. They adopt a public-be-damned attitude because they believe that their organization is entitled, by its very *raison d'etre*, to recognition. Ethically or even sociologically, this argument is not without some justification. Journalistically, however, it is noncompetitive and therefore without merit.

The professionals who raise money for schools, colleges, hospitals, and major charities recognize that theirs may be the purest public relations jobs that exist: the continued existence of the organization depends on their cleverness and continued success in image-building.

To enable smaller fund-raisers to compete with the giants, here are some approaches that might make the difference between operating as a tiny in-group and expanding every year to become a major community force:

1. Use your board of directors as a public relations implement. Who is on your board—simply some dedicated members? Either expand the board and seek out some added individuals whose value is the weight of their names, or keep the board as an operating entity and add a separate "board of governors" consisting of community leaders or local celebrities. The use of their names will add stature and press-worthiness.

2. If you have used telephoned pleas, pledge cards, theatre parties, and "Monte Carlo nights" so often that they deserve a merciful retirement, move your fund-raising into a different league. Stage a golf or tennis tournament—named after the most important person you can coerce into lending his name—and, once the tournament is announced (and not before, since the preliminary publicity helps spur activity),

get that person to help bring in celebrities. For example, you may talk the best-known television newsman in town into lending his name to the First Annual Joe Glutz Golf Tournament, which will be held at a local country club the last Friday in August. Joe Glutz is inextricably tied to the tournament once it is announced. *Then* you tell him, "Joe, we need your help. We must have half a dozen celebrities [sports personalities, show business people passing through town, or fellow television performers] to prime the pump, since we're charging three hundred dollars per person to play in a foursome that includes a celebrity."

Glutz must deliver or the event is a dud—which damages him more than it does you. If it is successful, the second year is 90 percent easier. By the way, promote prizes from local merchants, their names are printed in a program book. And if some people want to attend but not play golf, charge them fifty dollars, make card tables or putting greens available, and include them in the dinner afterward.

3. Stage a "King for a Day" luncheon or dinner. The event ostensibly is to honor a member of the organization or a supporter of the charity or an alumnus of the school. In reality, it is a fund-raising event. The "king" must be honored by "the largest turnout this town ever has seen," and in order for this to happen, modesty must go out the window. Anyone even remotely connected with the chosen "king" must be contacted and asked to take a table of ten. This procedure produces relief when the sights are dropped to a pair of tickets. At least one surprise speaker must be sought; the rostrum must include people of note and stature; and heavy publicity must accompany both the announcement of the King for a Day luncheon (or dinner), its progress, and its eventual staging—even to the point of reserving a table for the press. As with the golf or tennis tournament, if this event is handled with professionalism, making it an annual event will be a painless method of fund-raising.

4. Produce a television fund-raising commercial. If you decide to produce a spot, be sure to follow the rules of production outlined in Chapter 5. And be sure that the spot ends not with a generalized plea for funds but with a specific address to which donations should be sent. If you have theatrical connections, a 35mm fund-raising trailer can be produced for captive theatre audiences. In such a case, the trailer must end something like this: "And now we're asking the ushers to turn up the house lights for three minutes so that you'll have the opportunity to speak with your dollars as well as with your hearts for this important cause." Volunteers then pass canisters or baskets among the audience.

5. Mount a weekend "phone-a-thon" in which bright teenagers man a battery of phones for sixty consecutive hours, phoning for donations and pledges. Obviously, calls made during the middle of the night must be made cautiously to avoid public resentment; therefore, this group of calls is made to a preconditioned group of amiable people who have agreed to let themselves be called at 3:00 A.M. for the good of the promotion or because they are caught up in the publicity web. In order for the phone-a-thon to succeed, it must be publicized heavily beforehand; the community must know what the activity is and what the goals are. Calls must be salted with those who expect the call by prearrangement and whose response is geared to media coverage.

In every case, whatever steps are taken by the fund-raising group should be accompanied by notification to media. A change of officers, handing over a check (itself offering possibilities of both novelty and flair) to someone, or the staging of a special event, all are reasons for intensive cultivation of media coverage. Remember that special events offer only historical benefits afterward; difficult as it may seem, press coverage should be sought *before,* to help recruit people to attend.

In general, newspaper, television, and radio personalities

are excellent local candidates for the board of governors, for the namesake of a golf tournament, for king or queen for a day, and for on-camera spokesmen for the television fund-raising commercial. This is because they invariably have a fanatic core of followers who assure *some* success.

Using Embarrassment: A Dangerous Weapon

As fund-raising becomes more competitive and its techniques more sophisticated, schools and charities have begun to use a method that until the 1970s was used only by religious fund-raisers: embarrassment.

The technique of using embarrassment to help raise funds is tied closely to the public relations functions of publication. For example, a fund-raising organization will publish a list of "pledges." The purpose is not to glorify those who have pledged money, but to assure the organization that the checks will be forthcoming. The theory is that individuals who pledged to give money will see their pledge in print and therefore feel obligated to make that pledge good.

This technique is powerful when used within an organization, all the members of which receive the printed list, pamphlet, or book. It is more than powerful—it is stunningly objectionable—when such published information is sent to those outside the organization. One might argue, on behalf of those who do publish such materials, that publication is not verification of the pledge but merely recognition for that pledge. Further, the fund raisers say that the pledge was obviously made in good faith; therefore why should the person who made it object to having his name published? A theory of publicizing gifts is that publicizing one tends to generate gifts from others who see the publicity. A secondary benefit, however, is that the gift is "firmed" by the public exposure.

Occasionally, the entire approach to a major donor is couched in terms of publicity: "We're going to have a television crew on hand to film the signing of the check for your new building (or wing, etc.)." The subtle pressure brought to bear by publicity hardens the "deal." It can also speed by months the transfer of dollars, since the publicity has announced a timetable that otherwise was unstated.

Obviously, the danger of using embarrassment in these ways is that a peripheral group will drop away from the parent organization, sometimes in anger, because they feel that the group has taken a commercial direction. This is indeed the two-edged sword that can be a major problem in the sensitive area of fund-raising. However, most professional fund-raisers agree that embarrassment is their strongest weapon and that without it there is a group who would never fulfill their pledges—pledges that are given under pressure and that the individual has no intention of honoring until he sees his name in print.

The Telethon

Originated to raise funds for heavily organized groups, the telethon has in recent years been adapted for smaller groups, who negotiate with the television station to use from twenty-four to forty-eight hours of time in one continuous bloc.

As telethons become more popular, the inevitable result is that they become less and less professional, since invariably an in-group with little television production experience takes over both its organization and its operation.

An example of what can happen is the famous incident on the 1974 Democratic Party telethon, in which Senator Hubert Humphrey, who was supposed to introduce Senator Lloyd Bentsen, misread the cue cards and in addition to introducing Bentsen continued on to read the full text of Bentsen's speech.

But, except for the mammoth Jerry Lewis Muscular Dystrophy telethon, which has spread to more than 125 stations, the Democratic Party telethon has become perhaps the most successful such event; certainly it is the largest-scale annual "sponsored" telethon. First held in 1972, the telethon by 1974 resulted in phoned-in pledges of more than six million dollars. After eliminating those who failed to make their pledges good and production costs, including twenty-two hours on the ABC network for $2,500,000, the party realized a net of $2,900,000. Production cost of the 1975 telethon, held on a mid-July weekend, was $2,700,000. The combination of political and show-business personalities was lucky to hold its own that year, indicating not only that economic conditions were less favorable but also that a change in format might be considered.

Robert Strauss, Democratic Party chairman, reported that telethons supply about 40 percent of the entire budget of the Democratic National Committee and that between 1972 and 1975 the party's debt was reduced by about seven million dollars.

Birth of political telethons is usually credited to Barry Goldwater's Republican presidential campaign in 1964. During his campaign, a single televised show brought in several million dollars—and unleashed the floodgates for local and national politicians everywhere.

Typically, a television station will dedicate three cameras and its control room crew plus competent directors and producers. Rather than try to direct camera shots, the sponsor of the telethon should devote himself to lining up celebrities who will make the vehicle viewable. Too many telethons in the 1970s depend not on entertainment for their impact, but, erroneously, on their theme. However worthy a theme might be, it is no substitute for entertainment when the medium is television. Thus, we begin to see telethons with little entertainment value at all: instead, a group of dedicated individuals make speech after speech to what becomes a nonexistent audience. The donations they are able to acquire are in turn from the in-group they previously have notified.

It is indeed important to have a hard core of participants on the receiving end ready to go when your program goes on the air. Here is a means of handling this: The telephones are manned in two-hour shifts. Each shift consists of about eight to ten workers, and each of these workers has an individual responsibility to acquire "seed" telephone calls from friends, relatives, business associates, and anyone who owes a favor, is sensitive to the project or institution for which funds are being raised, or likes the mini-publicity of having his name mentioned on the air. These individuals are asked to call, on a special line whose number they are given, during the period when the volunteer is part of the on-the-air fund-raising panel. The phone number is a direct one to the desk manned by the volunteer: "Call me between 2:00 and 3:00 P.M. Sunday at this number, and I'll mention your name on the air."

Two purposes are served. First, those who have been given this instruction probably will call, if only out of a sense of obligation, and they will donate something because of the personal relationship that exists. Second, when calls are coming in, the effect becomes epidemic and others who might not have given if the phone calls were scanty will indeed give when they feel that many others recognize the validity and importance of the appeal.

Assuming that the telethon runs for twenty-four hours, twelve separate banks of ten each would mean 120 people on the telephone, and if each of these is able to persuade ten friends to call, you have 1,200 "seed" donations.

It is an oversimplification to suggest that the volunteers' friends will donate enough to make the tremendous work involved in mounting a telethon worthwhile. For that reason, outsiders must represent at least 80 percent of the total donations anticipated. One way to get outside donations is through the acquisition of celebrities to help publicize and run the telethon.

The best method is to have one major celebrity "front" the telethon from beginning to end; occasionally there is someone in the group whose relationship with a celebrity is strong enough to make a successful direct request. Otherwise, one should use every possible local disc jockey, newspaper columnist, politician, and show business personality. Disc jockeys are especially valuable since they are not usually visible and represent a source of talent that has the added benefit of on-the-air exposure on their own programs. The broadcast personalities will mention—usually many times—their forthcoming appearance on the telethon, which fattens the viewer base.

When putting together a telethon, an absolute schedule should be assembled, issued to all participants, and maintained. Performers should not be asked to arrive at the same time and have to wait, nor should there be long gaps with no entertainment. One should have local musical groups on hand to fill "holes" and to cover the inevitable nonappearance of some celebrity.

The organizers of the telethon should see to it that the "talent" is spread equally throughout the day and night. One error many make is to assume that their highest viewership will be during prime time hours. During prime broadcast time, the telethon is competitive with normal programming on other stations, which means that it competes against established viewer habits. It may well be that the 2:00 A.M. audience will be just as large as the 8:00 P.M. audience, since there is little competition at 2:00 A.M. This will be especially true if publicity covers the event properly, listing the lineup of talent through the night. Another benefit of listing the talent is that once verified in print there is less chance that these people will not arrive for their scheduled appearance.

Remember that show business personalities usually are not available from 7:00 P.M. until 1:00 A.M. except Monday.

It may pay to videotape segments of those unable to work with you on any other basis.

When using videotape and other station facilities, reach a clear understanding of what you may expect and what costs money. As more and more organizations attempt to mount telethons, stations (which occasionally are victims of semi-professionals) have begun to charge for everything not explicitly specified in the package. A station will tell the organization: "You can take over our facilities from 6:00 P.M. Saturday until midnight Sunday, but the charge will be $10,000, and all moneys you make are your own. That includes three cameras, three floormen, the control room and its crew, and Studio A. It doesn't include anything else."

What else might you want? Studio B for rehearsals. The phone switchboard. And videotape units. They undoubtedly will cost extra.

But that isn't the big decision. The big decision is whether the organization can raise enough money using this fund-raising device to justify the cost and effort. Those who simply want to see themselves on a studio monitor and have their friends see them on television will militate for the telethon; cooler heads may say that the number of dollars above the cost is too small to justify the tremendous time, expense, and, for that matter, risk. A theatre benefit, a ball, or a banquet might raise more money with less trouble and possible embarrassment.

Embarrassment also can stem from the introduction of too many ill-equipped people to the television cameras. Some people may "choke" on camera and stumble over lines; some may demand that their remarks be written on cards and then rivet their eyes on the words, never looking directly into the camera for fear they'll lose their place on the cards. Others may turn their allotted time into a sermon or use the forum to show off their erudition, becoming so pedantic that dials will turn all over the viewing area. Some will forget the purpose of the telethon and introduce (or worse, make in-joke references to) friends, relatives, and business associates, none of whom has a relationship with the project. Some will become maudlin and attempt to bring tears to the eyes of the viewers, succeeding only in bringing boredom. Some will introduce endless numbers of people, asking that the camera pan from individual to individual—not realizing that these people aren't "box office" to the viewers at home. Some will run far over their time, talking so long that fists will be waved wildly all over the studio (in the TV studio, the raised clenched fist means "end it!"). Some will introduce talent in such a flaccid, uncertain, or apathetic manner that the talent will become enraged, and some will introduce talent in such a florid manner that the viewers will become disgusted.

All telethons should be based on the reality of the television world—that the viewer is paramount. The dedication of the members of an organization is in no way transmittable to a viewer sitting at home. What that viewer is expected to do is make a donation, and this comes from repeated requests with telephone numbers, with the "seed" phone calls made by friends of those manning the phones, and by personal pleas from celebrities to their followers, fans, and believers.

Organization of the technical side of a telethon should be in the hands of one professional, who may (regrettably) be a hired hand. The advantage of having a dispassionate executive in charge is that he has a job whose success depends on professionalism and not on catering to officers of the organization, friends before whom he wants to show off, or semicelebrities to whom he may owe a favor. The professional means professionalism, and this is what too often is lacking in a local telethon.

The best time for the event seems to be a weekend, not only because members of the organization are available but also because the chances of all-night viewership are greater on a Friday or Saturday night.

The executive in charge should, first of all, complete the business arrangements with the station and with suppliers such as the telephone company. He should insist on a final master list of participants long before the program hits the air. This list will include not only those celebrities who have agreed to make an appearance, but also the people who will answer the phones.

He might, as well, in exchange for the attendant publicity and goodwill, negotiate with a local taxicab company to have its drivers pick up the pledges immediately from those who have made them. The collection rate will jump by many percentage points, since pledges made over the air are forgotten once the show is off the air, and since many people only want to hear their names on the air and will say anything to get that exposure.

Thus, the method is as follows:

When the pledge is received at the station, someone phones back to verify the pledge *before* the name is mentioned on the air. This eliminates false pledges. Then another group of volunteers (not necessarily those with contacts since their job is more mechanical) will call the cab company to have its drivers pick up the money pledged. As cab drivers arrive at the station with the donations, they (the cab drivers) can be put on the air. This not only validates the procedure but also makes these helpers into heroes and obviously into willing boosters.

Pledges from out of town usually must be taken on a trust basis, but the method of collection should employ professional collection procedures that are beyond the scope of this book. Whether by immediate pickup of pledges or another technique, one should enforce collection as dynamically as possible within the geographical area in which such collection is feasible.

The professional producer also schedules the talent at proper intervals. It may be that several groups will arrive at the same time, or that the mayor and a well-known newspaper columnist will arrive at the same time. Greeters should be on hand to welcome visitors and make them feel important. (They *are* important or they wouldn't have been invited to appear.) The professional organizer also will determine well in advance which musical numbers will be played by groups, to avoid the possible confusion and annoyance of having two groups play the same numbers.

Among the mandatory visuals is a graph-chart-thermometer showing the total collected so far. This is twice as effective if alongside is the projected desired total as of each hour or period. For example, at 2:00 A.M. we have collected $163,000. The projected number at this point was $146,000. We're over our projection.

By using this approach, the viewer is brought into the orbit of a contest in which he is a contestant—he is a helper in a triumph over odds. Someone may very well make that key donation to reach the goal at hand, whereas if the amount sought is unspecified, no one knows whether the final total is more or less than was expected.

One key to a successful telethon is the "Mighty Donation." The Mighty Donation comes from one individual—obviously someone of great means—who will equal an amount raised during a certain hour or who will donate a huge amount of money if a plateau is reached or who will make a spectacular offer on the air. When approaching people of means, the organizers of the telethon should make clear their intention to use an on-the-air mention as a primer to stimulate other viewers. The message will not be lost—that he will be a key celebrity himself before (hopefully) many thousands of viewers. If such a Mighty Donation can be arranged, it should be nurtured carefully, with small and delicate "leaks" given to the press and the announcement itself made by someone of as much consequence as those who run the telethon can obtain.

After the telethon is over, a steady stream of news stories should continue for some months. One of those stories might well refer to pledges that were not realized, which will stimulate some "conscience giving" and some "making good" of pledges by those who begin to think their names may appear in the newspapers if they don't. Some who otherwise had never heard of the telethon will send a check. Most stories should emphasize the success of the telethon, the results it has brought, the dedication of the money, the anticipated benefits to the community as a result of the telethon, and, most important, a look toward the following year.

Properly executed, a telethon will raise more money in less time than any other fund-raising method yet devised. Amateurishly run, it is a stigmatic blotch on the organization that will not disappear for months or even years.

Run your telethon—but do it professionally or suffer the consequences.

9

trade associations

The existence of trade associations in itself is an excuse for public relations activity.

Associations generally carry greater suggestions of importance and greater authority than can any individual company that might be a member of that association. For this reason, control of associations and control of the news disseminated by them has become in many cases a highly political matter. In fact, some associations are not associations at all but merely an extension of one individual who wants a seal of approval on information he releases.

For example, a company might award itself a certificate of excellence from a nonexistent association in its field, assuming that no one will bother to check the validity, the authenticity, or the existence of the association. Then the association or the recipient of the award issues a news release announcing the award. This is the kind of activity that does no legitimate association any good, but it is common enough to be noted.

One of the problems faced by assocations is equal space and equal coverage for all its members. Many associations have a dues structure weighted according to the dollar volume, number of employees, or net worth of each member. Obviously, the giant companies will pay a larger share of the operating expenses of the association, and one might think that they in turn are entitled to more attention from the association. This too can be a dangerous political ploy. Some years ago Metro-Goldwyn-Mayer threatened to withdraw from the Motion Picture Association of America if the film *Ryan's Daughter* was not rerated from "R" to "PG." The threat of withdrawal, many feel, resulted in the association's rerating the picture, and Metro-Goldwyn-Mayer remained in the ranks. However, the image of the association was damaged, and other members began to consider the technique of force and pressure as a negotiating tool.

Using Your Membership

In most associations, the president is not the operating head. He is the individual chosen or elected by the membership, who lends his name to activities and correspondence, but it is the paid executive secretary who effectively runs the association. Some executive secretaries reach positions of enormous power through their wheeling and dealing. Public relations activities of the association seem to be planned for their personal goal—to achieve a high personal profile in the press.

Anything that benefits the group benefits all members, but this platitude may never satisfy the small association member whose name is seldom seen on a news release and who is seldom represented in a panel, a seminar, or a television program on behalf of the association. Therefore, it behooves the member of an association to agitate (intelligently) for individual coverage. Here are some ways in which each member can do this:

1. Write letters to the executive secretary. By becoming a frequent commenter on association activities and on outside events that affect the association, members can reach the point of recognition that can spur association officials to consider their names in future plans for the association itself.

2. Circularize association board members with notes and letters. This invariably results over a period of a very few years in the individual's being invited to serve on that board, which represents a step up the public relations scale.

3. Make suggestions to committees. Individual members can, through written suggestions to committees with noted copies to the president and the executive secretary, show an apparent interest in the association which may very well result in that member's being called on to help execute future plans.

4. Volunteer to be a speaker. It is not enough to offer to give a speech at an association meeting or convention. One must suggest two or three topics that are of interest to the membership. If the association agrees to schedule the speech, it should not be taken lightly by the presenter, who should engage in the research, the polishing, and the methods of speech preparation described later in this chapter.

5. Circularize the entire membership. Occasionally a member will feel that his views on a particular development should be transmitted to the entire membership of the association. He may want action by the association in general; he may want his views promulgated on behalf of the association; or he may simply want his information to reach the other members. In such a case, a memo to members is businesslike and proper, provided the information in the memo does not look like a crackpot reaction or a thoughtless or unnecessary communication. Some associations, especially smaller ones, depend heavily on this kind of activity by their members for

the life of the association itself. In large associations, members might get such memos only once or twice a year.

Membership in an association can result in public relations benefits to the members as the direct result of membership (or even from the use of the association "seal" if stature can be suggested); conversely, members can give public relations benefits to their association.

News releases are one avenue of recognition: So-and-so has become a member, an officer, a speaker of the association, or he has attended the annual convention.

A second avenue is participation in association events. A third is recognition, originating in work done on behalf of the association. A fourth is the prestige stemming from membership in *any* association, which becomes part of a permanent personal background and biography.

These benefits are major reasons for joining an association in the first place; another is the acquisition of trade information and access to contacts.

Obviously, the best way to get public relations benefits from membership in an association is to work effectively and intelligently on behalf of that association. But it is naive to believe that without attention to the principles of public relations, attention will equal what can be achieved through a combination of effectiveness *and* public relations. But always remember that an obvious, inelegant demand for attention can stain a reputation and cause negative word-of-mouth publicity that can backfire and result in a polite but firm suggestion by a nominating committee to the effect that "this loudmouth should be dumped next year."

Making a Speech

The two great terrors of the amateur speechmaker go together: boredom and unprofessionalism.

Boredom in an audience, in fact, usually stems from unprofessionalism, since the professional speechmaker invariably builds into his speech fail-safe systems that rescue him when the warning signs go up.

What are the warning signs?

Beware when there is unusual coughing in an audience.

Beware when people begin to shift in their seats and do not sit attentively or at ease.

Beware when more than one person looks at his watch.

If your sensitivity is so poor that you miss these signs— signs clearer than a stoplight at the corner—you deserve the punishment of banishment from the rostrum, which will be the result unless your political or economic stranglehold over the group you are addressing is so powerful that you can force your way back to bore them again.

Professionalism in speechmaking is more than recognizing the signs of negative audience reaction; it obviously must include means of avoiding that reaction. Here is Lewis's "Unlucky Thirteen" list of *don'ts*:

Don't read lists of statistics. If they're essential to your speech, pass out printed statistical resumes beforehand and refer to the numbers without reading the whole list.

Don't try to wax poetic. Lifting lines from Shakespeare or the Bible is a tough exercise for the professionals. Any quotation of more than one sentence is suspect.

Don't shout. Talk conversationally. This enables you to use vocal volume for emphasis, which you can't do if you're yelling already.

Don't be afraid to be human. Pomposity breeds boredom.

Don't load your speech with phony jokes. If a joke falls naturally into place, great; if it doesn't, put a question mark alongside it on your notes and omit it if the audience isn't solidly with you by the time you come to it.

Don't make any speech longer than ten minutes unless everyone on hand knows that you're expected to speak for a longer time.

Don't go on cold. Rehearse your speech, perhaps while

driving your car—a great exercise since you have to keep going without constant reference to your notes.

Don't constantly look down at your notes throughout the speech. Establish eye contact with a different member of the audience for every sentence. By the time you're five minutes along, they'll all be yours, since they know they have to pay attention.

Don't end the speech on a flat note. A good speech builds to a smashing drum roll, a wave of the flag, and Abe Lincoln and Motherhood all rolled together.

Don't racehorse. Keep the pace flexible. A constant slow or fast pace is hypnotic because of its monotony; keep varying it. But too fast is worse than too slow because they'll miss half the words.

Don't sermonize. Dignity is a far better forensic tool than a false voice of God.

Don't stand statuelike. It's a wonderful ploy to wander (deliberately) away from the podium—even if you abandon the microphone—to make one telling point.

And the last is the toughest:

Don't write out every word. If you've written your speech word for word and lose your place, God help you. But if you're working from notes, enough naturalism and ad-lib comments will creep in to liven up the talk. And you won't feel glued to one place.

If you have to make a clever speech and can't think of anything clever to say, head for the library. You'll find a whole shelf of toastmasters' handbooks, funny sayings, topical jokes, and witticisms. You have two chores to perform: (1) Choose your ammunition carefully, being sure to avoid stale material, and (2) adapt the jokes to the situation in which the speech is being given.

An executive who gives speeches invariably is in many situations where he *hears* speeches. Carry a small note pad and jot down mannerisms, techniques, and even humorous material that appeals to you; if you like it, chances are that those who hear you will like it. This gives you a head start.

Now go knock 'em dead. But not for more than ten minutes.

10 PR projects for specific "hard" businesses

In this chapter and the next, we've listed some suggested publicity and public relations activities for specific businesses. The common denominator is that every one of them is a project you can do yourself, without professional counsel.

Your particular business may not be represented in any of the lists. You may, for example, be a bicycle dealer, unlisted here. All you need to do is check similar categories—motorcycle dealers, department stores, hobby shops—and determine which projects fit your business.

Remember, public relations, more than any other business except war and love (and we're no longer sure of those), is one in which you exist on your wits. Okay, let's start using them!

Apartment Buildings

1. Hold a party for all tenants. All media—print and broadcast—should be apprised of this unusual attempt to es-

111

tablish rapport between landlord and tenant. Announce this as a quarterly event. Your image will soar.

2. If a party is too rich for you, hold quarterly meetings, with opinions tossed back and forth. While there is some danger of a "bandwagon" effect, when one tenant may bring up an objection to management that the others would never have thought of had you not provided the forum, this gives you an opportunity to milk enormous publicity coverage, building image as you do. WARNING: If you're slow-witted don't try this.

3. In exchange for postings of local theatres, ask for passes. Give the passes to tenants on a rotating basis.

4. Prepare a news story in which you comment on the rental picture in your community. Include photographs of yourself and your property. The thrust of the story is that you hold two positions: (a) spokesman for apartment owners in general, and (b) the benevolent owner who is atypical of the breed.

5. If yours is a new development, hold a press luncheon to precede by two weekends (allowing for press deadlines) your grand opening. Use golf carts to show guests around the grounds.

6. For grand openings, have two types of celebrities on hand—one each to appeal to adults and children.

Audio-Visual Dealerships

1. Once a month, personally screen a film for an orphanage, a charity, or an off-the-street community group.

2. If you have a window that faces the street, set up a continuous projector to show innocuous films—cartoons or comedies. Passersby *will* stop to look.

3. Conduct a contest for the oldest film in town. You can run this on two levels: "home" movie films and theatrical films. Television personalities and/or newscasts will show the winners on the air if you approach them.

4. Sponsor a high school film-making contest. Offer an award to the best film. The key to this promotion is your acquisition of a panel of judges: local theatre owners, government officals, school principals or drama teachers, television personalities. The judges, as much as the contest, will gain press coverage for you. WARNING: Don't supply film-making equipment. You know why.

5. As new equipment is received, rewrite the news release or product information that may have come from the manufacturer and submit it as a straight news story, announcing a new audio-visual development, available from you. Be sure to include pictures with the story. If you're in those pictures, give yourself an extra point.

Automobile Dealerships

1. If you supply a car for a high school driver education class, be sure that it's throughly publicized. Have yourself photographed turning over the keys to the teacher.

2. Sponsor an antique car show. The entrants should display their cars on your lot over a weekend.

3. If you're in a college town, sponsor a student contest in automobile design. Properly structured, this promotion will gain you continuing press coverage from the moment you announce it until the moment you name the winner.

4. If a citizen has exceptional misfortune—his car is demolished or burned—offer him a month's use of a demonstrator. Acts of generosity such as this will go far to erase the typical car dealer image.

5. If there is national news regarding the automobile market, get on the telephone to newspapers and broadcast stations, giving them your views. For example, if a story states that car sales are down 10 percent, call to question the story and announce that your sales are up 15 percent. WARNING: Don't try to ad-lib. Have your statement prewritten so that your message is concise.

6. When new models are unveiled, invite community news media to a press preview, perhaps on the afternoon before the first public preview. Don't depend on factory publicity, which benefits competing dealers as much as it does you.

7. Your service department can establish an "executive limousine" to downtown for those who have left their cars. The difference between yours and the typical station wagon transportation is that your courtesy car is driven by a pretty girl, coffee is served, and a television set entertains passengers on their way to work.

Auto Parts Companies, Rentals, Ancillaries

1. The arrival of any new automobile accessory should be the basis of a news story to media. If the accessory is truly unusual, call the television stations for a demonstration. Samples to editors should be charged back to the manufacturer or supplier.

2. Whenever a visiting celebrity or dignitary arrives in town, make available one of your cars for his or her use. To prevent this from being private information, which will not benefit you, send notes to gossip columnists. A tiny and dignified—but visible—emblem on the trunk lid of the car should identify it as yours.

3. Popular disc jockeys may trade air mentions for use of a car. WARNING: This may work to your detriment unless you have a clear understanding. The car may be returned to you in undrivable condition or with 100,000 miles on it. Insurance is his responsibility, with a copy of the policy to you.

4. For your ten thousandth rental, carefully chosen, make a Rolls-Royce or a Mercedes-Benz 600 available to the renter. Charge Ford Pinto rates. Include a dinner at an exclusive restaurant. Photographic coverage of such an event is almost sure-fire. (It may be that you yourself will have to rent the car from another source; it's a worthwhile expenditure.)

5. Arrange to sell an exotic part for an antique car, and

set up a news story about the extent of your inventory and how far you will go to supply parts for any car. If you have parts for Edsels, DeSotos, Hudsons, Packards, or other obsolete makes, these can be touchstones for feature coverage of your real business.

Bakeries

1. One day a week, permit guided tours of the bakery if yours is a large one, or visits if yours is "boutique" size. Visitors receive something freshly baked, plus a printed history of the bakery and promotional materials.

2. Set up a luncheon for food editors and supply menus centering around your breads, rolls, cakes, or desserts for their columns. "New Recipes Using Bread" will help bring writers to the luncheon; the free meal will confirm.

3. Twice a year, singly or cooperatively with retail outlets, roll back prices. Publicize the event heavily.

4. For St. Patrick's Day, bake special green loaves using vegetable dye that will not affect the taste. A loaf is half price to anyone with an Irish name. Special wrapper bands identify the loaves. Invite television film crews and newspaper photographers to watch you personally, with green bowler and tie, bake the first batch, which will be delivered to the ranking Irish-descended politician.

5. Bake, in limited and controlled volume, "the most expensive bread in the world." These loaves must be special —in ingredients, appearance, and taste. Formal sealing wax and individual loaf numbers are in order. Use this bread for promotion, as gifts, and for special events, where the arrival and appearance of the bread soon will become a status symbol. (If you don't bake bread, make it a cake.)

6. Issue a feature story on your chief baker—or, if you're a one-person operation, on your own background. Emphasize gourmet aspects to separate yours from mass-production, impersonal bakeries.

Banks

1. Exhibit the works of local artists in the bank lobby. The exhibit changes monthly, as does the news release to local media about the artist being exhibited. WARNING: To avoid controversy, have artists selected by a committee of local experts.

2. Sponsor awards—for essays on Americanism, for drawings, paintings, and sculpture, for sports. The awards, made as publicly as possible, will gain significance if properly publicized.

3. Write a news story to financial media whenever a personnel appointment of any consequence is made.

4. Any bank news is worthy of a news story to media: higher interest rates, premiums to savings depositors, a new type of savings account.

5. Comments on national economic news often are welcomed by media if they are made by a high official of a local bank. Even though these comments may mirror those of more important national figures, the local angle makes them newsworthy.

6. A newsletter on national and local business conditions can be a potent public relations weapon if handled thoughtfully. These can be mailed with bank statements, sent to all media, placed on counters in the lobby, and used to acquire new business.

7. Promotion-minded bankers can invent reasons for news coverage: the twenty thousandth depositor, reaching a new high in assets, new landscaping.

8. Special deals on checking accounts for teen-agers (whose parents have accounts in the bank) will win friends and influence people.

9. A special service window, which sells stamps, handles telegrams, and operates as a message center at times of

disaster, is a community service that pays off in public attitude.

10. Offer the public a free map of the city or the metropolitan area. Not only does this bring them into the bank, but your name on the map will be a constant image-builder. Media will give coverage to the issuance of the map.

11. Arrange for someone to deposit a huge cache of pennies—perhaps a thousand dollars' worth. A prior tip will bring out all media for news coverage, especially if the pennies are carried in an odd vehicle—an armored truck, the trunks of half a dozen cars, or a rented trailer (for which you graciously pay).

Beauty Salons

1. One of the strongest public relations moves that can be made in this wild and woolly business is to get a regular column in a community newspaper—beauty hints, tips on hair styles, or trends in makeup. The significance of such a column is not to be taken lightly, and therefore preparation must never be slapdash. For original editorial consideration, the first half-dozen columns should be presented to the feature editor.

2. New hair styles might be interesting enough to bring out reporters and television crews if they're made to seem trendy or if they're tied to sociological change.

3. If there is a legitimate theatre in town, arrange to set the hair of visiting stars.

4. Some schools will cooperate in beauty clinics held by beauticians whose own reputations grow if only because they have conducted the clinics.

5. Ask local clubs and organizations—even those of which only men are members—if they'd like a speech. Give the speech a strong title—"Get Your Kicks from Curls" or "He'll Kiss More Than Your Cheek If . . ." and your acceptance ratio will go up.

6. A beauty newsletter can bring new customers, especially since timing is so important in motivating potential customers in this field.

7. Whenever a new stylist is appointed, award a certificate to him or to her as an "accredited stylist." Publicize the appointment heavily to build your reputation as well as the stylist's. The certificate, framed, hangs in the shop.

Beverage Distributorships

1. Rename your flavors to give them some glamour. It isn't just "cherry"—this month it's "big black cherry" and next month it's "very berry cherry." Flavor names are a sound base for image-building to give your brand uniqueness.

2. Every visitor should receive a commemorative can. This applies to salesmen, children, workmen—anyone who comes into the bottling plant. The commemorative can differs from a regular can in color (perhaps gold) but the content is identical.

3. Use commemorative cans also when supplying soft drinks for charity events, for civic celebrations, and for giveaways.

4. Prepare a float for local parades. The obvious design is a can or bottle or both. The float can tour the streets between parades and can become a well-known local symbol. Miniatures of the float, and plastic inflatables using the same design, are perfect premiums.

5. Negotiate with ice cream manufacturers for a local "soda month." Tie-ins with each other's advertising are only one facet; point-of-sale is another. A "sodamobile" can tour the streets. At random, free sodas are given to passersby or delivered to the nearest house.

6. Beer distributors can sponsor a beer-drinking contest, with the winner crowned Beer King. Public appearances are implicit, which means that entrants in the contest must sign releases beforehand (see Appendix).

7. Also for brewers: arrange to have someone halfway across the world demand your beer. It should be shipped as ostentatiously as possible and promoted in advertising as well as news stories.

Book Stores

1. Using the methods described in Chapter 5, negotiate with the programming department of local television shows for a regular program—"The World of Books." Be prepared to videotape several sample shows. WARNING: The great danger in the world of books is "bookishness"—the tendency to become pedantic, dry, dull, pompous, and boring.

2. Negotiate with newspapers to become a book reviewer. They may well remind you that you are a competitor, commercially, with other book dealers; your reply need be nothing beyond bright, witty, informative book reviews prepared as samples. WARNING: *Reread* the warning issued for the previous point.

3. Become the focal point of literary events. If an author comes to town, interview him (free-lance if necessary) and then submit the article to local publications. If well-written, such articles can be a ticket to a permanent assignment. Failing all else, use the interview(s) as the basis for a regular newsletter, distributed to customers and the press and left on your counter as free reminder-advertising.

4. Capitalize on events. Become chairman of the Hemingway Centennial Committee, which can be milked for years; organize businessmen and educators for a Read-a-Book Week; sponsor annual writing awards for high school and college students—with occasional controversy over some selections.

5. Donate a thousand leftover books to the local library. Acts of generosity, heavily publicized or not, are valuable to your image.

6. Become involved in causes; be known as an innova-

tor. One week, feature comic books—those that tell classic stories such as *The Last of the Mohicans* or *Macbeth*. Another week, offer a Generation Gap Special: a rock record and a classical record, sold in combination. "Sponsor" an author whose book you appreciate but is not selling well. WARNING: Don't become known as an oddball.

Bridal Shops

1. Prepare a speech on "The Perfect Wedding" and offer it to schools and clubs. Weddings are like cross-country moves or funerals: they're not everyday occurrences, but when they do occur it's a major event and most people want to do business with professionals.

2. Prepare a booklet on wedding etiquette—factual, not just rhetoric—and send a copy to every family that has announced their daughter's engagement. Excerpts from this booklet form a logical base for a newspaper column or a radio or television interview.

3. Set up window displays, each week featuring a different kind of wedding. Get ethnic and interest-group help; these helpers will publicize their work. Be sure to include the guitar-playing, barefoot type of wedding, with some clever touches of your own. Such inclusions build image with young people, who are, after all, the basis of the bridal shop business.

4. Using a permanent Polaroid camera setup, offer photographs to each bride-to-be of herself in each gown or outfit she tries on. These won't be discarded and can result in favorable word-of-mouth publicity and greater business volume from each customer.

Bus Lines

1. Set up special local tours to coincide with seasons. For example, a Halloween "haunted house" evening, in which a busload of fun-seekers visit supposedly haunted houses, decaying old cemeteries, and eerie areas, is pressworthy if it

shows some thought: black cats prowling through the bus; a witch, picked up as a hitch-hiker; sound effects.

2. Most bus lines offer special fares to students, senior citizens, and policemen. Few think of special days for other groups. Examples: a half-fare day (or morning) on runs to the beach or half fare whenever the temperature is above 95 degrees; half fare to anyone carrying an American flag (or, on ethnic holidays, a flag or costume of the country involved) special buses to rock concerts, featuring rock background music.

3. Issue statements relative to energy conservation, whether asked for them or not. Any attempt to make the community conscious of mass transportation is a true community service.

4. Invite students to decorate a bus—for a historic event, for holidays, for civic events. WARNING: Be sure to use cardboard, paper, or removable paint.

5. Working in concert with a sports team, an auditorium, or a theatre, provide transportation to a game or performance, for senior citizens, orphans, or underprivileged children. Participations such as these make good gossip-column items.

6. Display a brand-new bus at shopping centers or in the center of town. The bus is open for the public to walk through; youngsters may sit at the wheel. Be sure to distribute booklets showing routes, rates, availabilities for charter, the history of the omnibus, or local history.

Camps

1. A standard news release, which requires only insertion of the name of the child and parents, should be prepared for newspapers in every community from which campers are recruited. (Use only one release per community, listing all campers from that area in the same release.)

2. Make all campers members of the Camp Alumni As-

sociation and hold a reunion during the winter. To assure attendance, award many prizes at the reunion. Be sure to take photographs.

3. Invent for yourself an area of expertise. Contribute an article to *any* publication, whether oriented to parents, to the camping industry, or to a peripheral area such as food preparation or sports activities. Reprints of the article should be mailed to parents of all campers and prospective campers, with an appropriate covering letter. A news release announcing publication of the article should be sent to local media.

4. If budget permits, make a film—not a film glorifying your camp, but one showing a city child having pleasant exposure to nature, or showing emotional development, or emphasizing interpersonal relationships: "Four Weeks Can Change a Lifetime" or any cosmic title. You can build a following on the local lecture circuit, and on television interview shows, with that film. If you shoot in 35mm rather than 16mm, you can offer it as a free short subject to local motion picture theatres. WARNING: If your film is a piece of self-puffery, expect it to bomb, which it should.

5. In each shopping neighborhood, negotiate with a merchant to sponsor a child for camp. Distribute materials for a contest run through that store; the winner receives two or four weeks at camp. The contest might be an essay, a letter, a drawing, an achievement, a recommendation by a parent or friend, or a blind drawing. Cost to the merchant is nominal, and you and he will share the publicity.

Carpet Cleaners

1. In front of your premises, lay red indoor/outdoor carpet. As an attention-getting device, the red carpet suggests many promotional ideas.

2. Each week, exhibit a piece of carpet. Invite the public to stain it with mud, jelly, oil, and half-finished drinks.

Then clean the carpet. If the piece has been pretreated properly, it'll clean well.

3. Celebrate cleaning the hundred thousandth or one millionth yard of carpet by offering the winner a free carpet cleaning. And, to assure press coverage, take the winning family out to dinner.

4. If you have a large cleaning machine, give it a name such as the "X-20" or "Magicleaner" and submit a feature story on the machine and what it does.

5. Negotiate for an appearance on a television show to discuss carpet cleaning. In telling homemakers how to remove stains, you can point out that some stains must be handled professionally.

Catering Businesses

1. Contact food editors relative to establishing a regular column, "Cooking for Company" or "Serving a Mob." This column will differ from standard recipe columns in that it is geared to mass food preparation and does not limit itself to ingredients; it includes the philosophy, the niceties, and the technical aspects of bulk food preparation.

2. Establish a local dessert-preparation contest. Choice of judges in itself can be a source of strong press coverage. The winning dessert, properly (and provocatively) named, will be added to your permanent menu for five years. If the name of the dessert includes the winner's own name, expect many referrals.

3. Issue a news story announcing establishment of a special "haute cuisine" division, to be the ultimate in gracious gourmet service. If you plan your menu choices carefully, calling you to cater an event can become the "in" thing to do.

4. When catering a party, ask the hostess if she would like you to handle coverage in the society pages. If she agrees, submit a news release that also mentions your name as ca-

terer. IMPORTANT: Allow the hostess to inspect the news release and make no promise that it will be printed.

Clothing Stores

1. For special events, stage a costume-piece fashion show—a "Roaring Twenties" or "Turn of the Century" or "2001" show that, with a reasonably bright commentary, will win much recognition. By asking members of women's clubs to model, you'll get extra publicity mileage.

2. Prepare a float for the Memorial Day, July Fourth, Homecoming, or Thanksgiving parade. Exhibit current fashions on a large turntable.

3. Have a semiannual showing for the press. Don't worry about duplicating what is done nationally: yours is a local event. Include both men's and women's clothing if you carry both. IMPORTANT: Always have at least one highly controversial item.

4. Stage a fashion show once a year at the high school, using students as models.

5. Present a hat, a tie, a shirt, or a sweater to the local athlete of the week. Or, if the local team wins a championship, give them all matching ties or sweaters.

6. Sponsor a high school fashion creation contest. The winner will have her (or perhaps his) work exhibited in the store and will win a spring or fall outfit.

Contracting/Developing Operations

1. Having a celebrity on hand for a grand opening or an open house is a tested and sure way to build traffic. Be sure to release publicity in time for press coverage; try to time coverage as close to the actual date as possible, but not so late that prospective buyers will have made other plans.

2. Invite a dignitary—mayor, governor, congressman, or senator—to plant the first tree. The overtones of tree-

planting are far more positive and beneficial than standard ground-breaking.

3. If you have a development, resist the urge to name streets after your family, and instead use pressworthy names. Don't be so topical that names become obsolete. One key street or square can be preannounced as an annual name-changer, provided there are no residential addresses that will have to be changed each year. One year, with appropriate ceremonies, it might be (*Sports Hero*) Square; the next year, (*Motion Picture Star*) Square; the next year, (*Famous Author*) Square. Avoid controversy, and don't award the name until you're assured your nominee will appear at the ceremonies.

4. A press luncheon is a proper vehicle for announcing a new development, a new building, or a renovation of a major property. WARNING: Don't invite the press only to give them "pygmy information" about nothing very much.

5. Issue news releases quoting you on the state of the housing industry in your market. Over a period of time, this will establish you as spokesman for the industry.

6. Bury a time capsule in the cornerstone of a building under construction. On parchment, give the library and all other logical organizations instructions and a list of contents. A high school contest can precede the actual installation of the capsule, with students suggesting items to be included.

Department Stores

1. The store's windows are loaded with public relations potentials. At high school or college homecoming time, invite students to decorate a window; have an occasional "live surprise" in one window; stage a weekly fashion show in the largest window.

2. At the holidays, install "the world's largest electric train." The train, on brightly painted two-by-four trestles

above normal reach, can circle and crisscross the main floor or be even more intricate. Prizes to children can include a chance to be the "engineer," manning a carefully controlled throttle. A dump car on the train occasionally can release discount coupons or candy. All media will respond to this promotion: electric trains are universally appealing.

3. Continuous excitement can be generated by issuing a numbered ticket to each customer. At some previously unannounced moment, a celebrity draws the winning ticket, which is good for a color television set for one cent.

4. As seasonal fashions arrive, negotiate with a local television station to show the new fashions on a women's program or newscast. If there is no television station in town, the editor of the newspaper should be approached to run a prewritten feature on new styles.

Dog Kennels

1. Sponsor a local dog show, offering prizes for best of breed, including mixed breeds. WARNING: If you give the impression that you're simply patronizing the youngsters and don't take the event seriously, no one else will take it seriously. Arrange to be sanctioned by some official body, whether kennel association or local government.

2. Submit "Care of Your Pet" columns to the local newspaper. These columns should discuss cats, parakeets, and other locally common pets as well as dogs.

3. Negotiate to have yourself interviewed on broadcast programs, discussing both interesting anecdotes about the world of pets and more serious and controversial topics (for example, "Should Dogs Be Spayed?").

4. Offer public service radio announcements to local stations (for example, "Keeping Your Pet Comfortable in Hot Weather").

5. On the lower secondary school levels, take pets to class and give talks about pets. You'll not only be *the* recog-

nizable name as these youngsters get older; you'll also sell pets and supplies.

Employment Agencies

1. Issue a weekly "Job Index," which, as closely as possible, mirrors the job market for that week on four levels: unskilled, office, blue collar, and white collar. An "Executive Job Index" can be a separate undertaking. Copies should be sent to all news media as well as clients and prospective clients; appearance should be professional, not promotional.

2. Using the Job Index as a springboard, work with community newspapers to establish a column, "Your Job." This column should explain job opportunities, tell readers what various jobs pay and what background and experience are required, and avoid any overt mention of your own agency except in peripheral examples.

3. A monthly newsletter can explain job trends and make you the spokesman for all employment agencies. Some of the competition may object or may copy you, but this is to be expected whenever a positive business move is made.

4. Announce innovations, even if you already are using some of the methods you describe: for example, a new aptitude test for applicants, with some of the more stimulating types of questions suggested as "teasers"; creation of special departments, such as "Computer Force" or "Top-Level Recruitment"; computerized protection for job-changers to avoid sending applications to places they don't want such applications to go. All these are logical subjects for news releases.

5. Announce a hot-line phone number that will list job availabilities late into the evening. The hot line should give a fast-action impression.

6. Print a pamphlet, "How to Find *Your* Job." If done in a no-nonsense, informative way, with a minimum of personal puff and a maximum of hard information, it will be in demand by school placement offices as well as by individuals.

The pamphlet also is a strong introduction for yourself as a speaker to groups.

Finance Companies

1. Publicly make cash awards to police and fire heroes. This is community service and builds a reputation for both largesse and availability.

2. Make a public service announcement that in case of any local disaster, your company will permit a moratorium on loans due. This applies not only to floods and tornadoes, but also to major fires and epidemics.

3. Establish a series of money management clinics, with "name" speakers if possible. These clinics can be held in your offices (with refreshments and gifts such as paperback books), union meeting halls, schools, or clubs. If there is real meat in the sessions, they'll be in demand.

4. Publicize the "Ten-Minute Loan." This, and any other local innovation you can institute, is worthy of comment in the financial pages and often represents a genuine news story.

Florist Shops

1. Offer yourself as speaker to local clubs and groups. Include stimulating speech titles in your suggestions: "Roses in December," "Grow a Ten-Inch Orchid in Your Kitchen," "The New Look in Corsages."

2. Give a "Green Thumb Award" at fairs and shows. The award is given to the grower of the best plant or flower, or to the greenest lawn, or to the prettiest floral arrangement, or to the best painting or photograph of flowers. In addition to the award, a plaque or trophy will assure you that the winner will be a permanent salesman.

3. Donate flowers to a nursing home each week. WARN-ING: Don't *over*donate. If you have too great a reputation

of openhandedness, people will hate you when you *don't* donate flowers.

4. Whenever possible, participate in street parades. Your float need be nothing more than a flat-bed trailer heavily covered with flowers and perhaps including "Miss Roses" or "Miss Carnation."

5. Establish an annual World of Flowers contest. Give seeds to school classes. The best flowers grown from these seeds win a prize.

6. Show exotic and even controversial plants in a special place in the window—for example, a Venus' flytrap or ginseng. If the plants are hard to import or identify, so much the better. Invite television cameramen to film the plants—a good prospect if the plants open and shut (such as the Venus' flytrap trapping and digesting an insect).

Formal Wear Stores

1. Issue local "best dressed" awards. If you're brave, also issue "worst dressed" awards. You need not have permission to pick winners and losers, and this event confirms your authority in the world of men's fashion.

2. Stage a high school fashion show, exhibiting men's formal wear that will be in style for this year's prom. WARNING: High school students have a tendency to clown it up. Be sure to conduct the show with reasonable dignity. Each male model should be accompanied by a "date," which will help both visual interest and basic dignity.

3. Supply a free tuxedo for the prom king.

4. In your window, show unusual items: "The world's most expensive formal jacket," with precious stones and gold thread; occasional live models; old jackets to show the history of formal wear.

5. The history of formal wear is also a natural for a booklet, pamphlet, or one-shot newspaper story. Also to be

included, to make the booklet valuable, is a list of do's and don'ts.

6. When a new style arrives, have a press preview. Even though your premises may not be ideal for showings, conduct the preview with flair. Offer cocktails; have your own personnel dressed formally; and supply press kits. To assure adequate attendance, either have invitations delivered personally by formally clad messengers or expand your basic media list to include every remotely possible outlet—the high school and parochial press, disc jockeys, house organ editors.

Furniture Stores

1. Donate game tables to nursing homes. (Obviously, this is a goodwill gesture toward those who never will be your customers.) A sample of the table, with an appropriate sign, is a good prospect for a window display.

2. Sponsor a rocking chair contest, perhaps for the *Guinness Book of World Records*. Whoever rocks the longest wins his chair, plus an annual award—a challenge and a natural source of publicity a year hence.

3. Offer a free Christmas tree with any fifty-dollar purchase. Your store's Santa Claus will deliver surplus trees the day before Christmas to needy families or appropriate charities.

4. Twice a year, stay open for a twenty-four-hour day and have a housecleaning of all surplus furniture. Have bands, specials, and excitement, and serve breakfast at 4:00 A.M. This event will require coordination of publicity with media advertising.

5. In your window, exhibit waterbeds together with conventional mattresses. At high-traffic hours, have a live model "sleep" in the bed. Arrange to have this model interviewed about the waterbed experience.

Furriers

1. Outfit a bus or recreational vehicle as a "furmobile." This vehicle can be used promotionally in fairs, parades, and suburban shows and as a means of actually selling furs. In addition to furs themselves, display promotional and explanatory photographs and literature.

2. Arrange with a local restaurant—preferably an expensive one—to show furs during lunch one day a week. The restaurant will help publicize the fur fashion shows.

3. Occasionally use a live model on a slowly rotating turntable in the window

4. A furrier once capitalized heavily on a "mistake" in which he advertised a fur coat for "1,500 potatoes." Someone arrived with 1,500 potatoes and demanded the coat. The furrier protested, loudly and publicly, that the radio commercial in which the coat was advertised made it clear that "potatoes" meant dollars. Ultimately, he delivered the coat for the potatoes—with many thousands of dollars in free publicity.

5. As a means of publicizing an early sale, send two or three models to the beach wearing fur coats with bikinis underneath. You may get lucky and have photographs picked up by the wire services.

6. Arrange an armed guard for an especially expensive coat. The guard himself should wear a fur.

Gasoline Service Stations

1. Celebrate the sale of the one millionth or ten millionth gallon of gas. Anticipating this, it should be no great problem to sell that gallon to the mayor or to a celebrity, perhaps driving a car of the year in which the station opened.

2. One day each week, use female gas station attendants.

3. Hire a female to clean windshields.

4. Approach newspapers and broadcast stations to

carry a "Care of Your Car" feature, written by you and/or featuring you.

5. For one day, roll back the prices to some historic date—the end of World War II, the day you opened the station, the day you were born.

Groceries/Supermarkets

1. Schedule wine-tasting parties for customers. Such parties can be held in the evening, after the store normally is closed, and an expert can discuss various wines and offer samples. Aside from the business that can be generated, the event invariably is pressworthy.

2. For youngsters, offer a soft drink-tasting party. The method parallels that of a wine-tasting party; prizes can be awarded for the best palate—ability to recognize Coca-Cola, Pepsi-Cola, Royal Crown Cola, and other brands.

3. Print a weekly "Budget Menu Planner" offering recipes for nourishing but inexpensive meals. Offer specials on the ingredients. The recipes should be offered to food editors, and you should attempt to have weekly broadcast coverage, perhaps as an insert in a feature or interview program.

4. Issue a weekly list of best buys and worst buys. Try to be honest, because you'll find little negative effect on sales and much positive effect on image. For example, if sugar, cocoa, bacon, or bread has risen in price, put it on that week's list of worst buys. If chicken, soft drinks, bananas, or milk drops in price, put it on that week's list of best buys. Issue an advance copy of the list to all media. You may find yourself becoming a regular on a broadcast program one day a week.

Health Food Stores

1. Either as a newspaper feature or a one-minute broadcast feature, put together a "Daily Health Tip." Obviously,

the tip should be food-oriented; obviously, too, it should never openly promote you.

2. On a fine summer day, set up tables outside the store and serve, free or for two cents, "health food cocktails." If you charge the two cents, donate the money to a charity.

3. Invite a television reporter to visit you for a meal, 2001-style. The meal will consist entirely of health foods, carefully selected (with some research) for nourishment and satisfaction as well as taste.

4. Debunk something. It might be an aphrodisiac, or a sidebar to the cholesterol controversy, or a commentary on synthetic versus natural vitamins.

5. Arrange with a local athletic hero to live entirely on Tiger's Milk or any other such food for one week. At the end of that week, in a press conference or luncheon, your hero will lift weights, do push-ups, or perform some task that obviously requires strength.

Hobby Shops

1. Build the world's biggest or longest something—electric train, miniature car raceway, toy-size waterway. Open this exhibit only during rigidly controlled hours, and prior to the public opening have a press preview.

2. One evening a week, have a workshop in which you supervise, free, construction of models bought from you. This leads to suggestion 3.

3. Annually, sponsor a model exhibition, open to any airplane, motorcar, train, or spaceship under five feet long. You'll need cooperation from schools, scout troops, and clubs to make this as big as it can become. Exhibit the winning model in your window for a month and write an article for a trade magazine featuring that model; the coverage in the trade magazine will result in additional local coverage.

4. Cooperatively with the nearest airport if possible, sponsor an annual model plane show. Other merchants will

cooperate in supplying prizes for the longest sustained flight, the best aerobatics, and best takeoffs and landings. A prize for the largest model will be a better publicity bonanza each year, as the models expand in size to beat the biggest of the year before.

Hotels and Motels

1. If the name of your hotel or motel is not prominently displayed in every meeting room, be sure to cover that oversight immediately. Any publicity photographs or film footage shot in those rooms will then include the name.

2. Establish a "Businessmen's Thirty-Minute Lunch" in one of your dining rooms and invite the press and broadcast reporters to sample it. The approach is: "In at 12, out at 12:30." And make it work.

3. Under special conditions, offer a free room. This is especially pressworthy when it's an act of mercy or compassion. Example: a family is burned out of its home; you supply a room for three days. WARNING: Don't overdo this or you'll be expected to supply a room whenever anyone has a fire.

4. To hotel/motel trade publications, submit "How I Solved It" columns. These can result in national coverage and recognition.

5. Offer a due bill to any columnist or commentator who makes positive mention in the press or on the air.

6. Reintroduce the "continental tradition"—shining guests' shoes overnight, serving a "civilized" cup of coffee in the morning—any service that you can supply without incurring ridiculous cost. And be unflappable. Word-of-mouth can only help promote and publicize.

Insurance Agencies

1. Unusual risks are your best source of press coverage. Whether it's a singer's voice, a pet, or a no-rain picnic policy, the press will like it. As mentioned earlier, in some cases

you must publicize without revealing your client's identity. People in show business, on the other hand, often will not only welcome publicity; they'll help you get it. Therefore:

2. Working with a theatre owner, insure patrons for one million dollars against heart failure as they watch a horror film or against passing out cold during a torrid love scene. You'll get press coverage. WARNING: Don't be too sophomoric, or your promotional stunts can backfire.

3. Publish a monthly newsletter discussing trends and availabilities in coverage. Don't make this hard-sell, or no one will read it. Keep it informative.

4. Publicize any awards won by you or anyone in your office. Most insurance companies cooperate willingly in the issuance of awards to agents and brokers. Discuss this with your own source, helping to establish awards if none exists. An award for service or award for excellence is better than a "million dollar" award, because the latter is obviously and purely commercial.

5. If your parent company is uncooperative, establish intramural awards for excellence and service. Make these awards as publicly as possible.

Jewelry Stores

1. Display the world's largest fake diamond. The gem itself should have some visual appeal and not look like a big piece of glass. Perhaps a synthetic diamond house will cooperate.

2. For the high school prom, underwrite a "Cinderella" contest and permit the winner to wear a tiara or necklace of substantial worth. (Obviously, some security must attend this event.)

3. Offer jewelry, for wearing purposes only, to a local female television personality in exchange for occasional mentions on the air. (Again, take security precautions when loaning items of great value.)

4. Proclaim local Emerald Month or Sapphire Month.

In addition to window displays and promotion tie-ins with other stores, conceal a gem somewhere in the city. Have a local disc jockey release rhymed clues to the location; a continuing list of such clues, as mentioned on the air, will be posted in your store. Ultimately a winner will claim the gem. While the amount of other media publicity will be in ratio to the value of the stone, remember that the promotion itself is worthless if the stone is nearly so.

Landscaping Companies

1. Put together a factual, easy-to-read booklet with a title such as "How to Beautify Your Grounds." Make copies available in retail outlets (lumberyards, lawn furniture stores), to customers, and as a heavily publicized free offer.

2. Using the booklet as original background and ammunition, propose a seasonal newspaper column or radio commentary on grounds beautification.

3. Sponsor an annual award for the community's most beautiful landscaping. If your judges have some stature and the award isn't loaded in your own favor, the award will quickly become significant and highly pressworthy.

4. Call local clubs and organizations and offer your services as speaker: "Ten Low-Cost Tips for Landscaping" or "Only God Can Make a Tree but You Can Plant It."

Laundries, Cleaners, and Dyers

1. To all babies born on an anniversary date, offer free diaper service for three months.

2. Celebrate the ten millionth garment to be washed; invite the press to follow this garment through the various processes. Ultimately, buy it from its owner and display it in a frame or shadow-box.

3. Offer to launder or dry clean American flags free. The offer should be made a week or so before holidays on which the flag is displayed.

4. Twice a year, donate all unclaimed garments to a charity. Since you're inviting the press to cover the event, be sure all items donated are clean and in relatively good condition.

Liquor Stores

1. Wine-tasting sessions are naturals for liquor stores. Have such parties by invitation, with gifts and discussions led by a local authority (perhaps a knowledgeable salesman of your own).

2. For a fund-raising event, invite local columnists, food editors, celebrities, disc jockeys, and entertainers to participate in an "Identify the Scotch" contest. Each contestant will be asked to sip five brands of scotch and identify them; the closest guess results in a donation to the charity of the contestant's choice.

3. At holidays, buy broadcast time for public service announcements advising the public to avoid overindulgence and to avoid driving after drinking. While the broadcast spots will be paid for, the move itself is public relations in action. Inevitably, both image and press recognition result.

4. Acquire, preferably from a foreign source, a truly ancient bottle of wine or brandy—perhaps a century old. Arrange to open this bottle (and be prepared to supply some entertaining folklore about it) on a television show, where you'll pour it for the host and the guests. Comment on the taste, even if that comment is negative; you'll put yourself in the position of expert. (Wines and brandies are better than hard liquors for this event, because they have fewer detractors.)

Motorcycle Dealers

1. Sponsor rallies and road races. Winners receive trophies and recognition. Advise sports editors of the event, and call the television stations to let them know, since motorcycles are highly visual.

2. Ask the high schools for an opportunity to speak on "Motorcycle Safety." They'll make the time available.

3. One evening a week, from 5:00 to 7:00 P.M., hold a do-it-yourself repair seminar. The seminar should be structured rather than unstructured—that is, each session attacks a single topic, with you or your mechanic as demonstrator. (Left unstructured, the sessions deteriorate into a simple free use of tools.)

4. Offer a leading disc jockey three months' free use of a motorcycle, provided that your name appears on it in some prominent area and provided that occasional on-the-air mentions are made. The business this will bring is well worth the wear and tear on the cycle.

5. Ask a supplier for a special cycle that you can display for a week or two. This can be a heavily chromed or specially painted cycle, an extraordinarily powerful cycle, or a cycle that was used by Evel Knievel or some other celebrity.

Moving Companies

1. Line up a project that represents "the most" of something—the most expensive piece of furniture, the most softballs or tennis balls or theatre chairs or flowers—ever moved in your community.

2. To prove the cushioned care of your vans, serve a formal lunch in the van to a family at the same time their household goods are being moved. If you pull out the stops and use waiters in formal dress, serving vintage champagne, you'll earn a lot of press coverage.

3. Celebrate publicly your five-thousandth, ten-thousandth, or fifty-thousandth move.

4. Award plaques of recognition to your own employees for safety or service. Awards ceremonies not only build goodwill but also are strong press-release materials.

5. Arrange with a florist to deliver flowers or a plant to each family the night after their move, or send over a bucket of fried chicken and some expensive ice cream. These

touches are pure public relations, without the immediate press benefits of "stunts," but the word-of-mouth publicity will pay off, perhaps in media coverage at some point.

6. The U.S. Government requires that interstate movers supply a printed performance record to clients. Accompany yours with another printed piece, of the same size—commendations from people you have moved.

Music Stores

1. Sponsor a semiannual musicale, featuring musicians of many age brackets (under six, six to ten, eleven to fifteen, sixteen to twenty-one, over twenty-one, over forty-five, and over sixty-five). Give certificates to all participants.

2. Once a month, open the store for a Saturday Night Special, when contemporary popular music is played and specials are offered. Serve nonalcoholic punch and reserve an area for dancing. Have high school sports figures and leaders as in-house disc jockeys. Parents can be on hand as observers (monitors). WARNING: Don't allow unlimited attendance. Issuing invitations and/or controlling attendance will prevent bedlam and perhaps physical damage that can ruin the evening.

3. Let customers vote for the rock group of the month; each month's winner will be featured the following month in window displays. Contact the record company for a statement or recorded comment from the winner. A written thank-you can be blown up and displayed in the window; a recorded one can be dubbed and sent to local radio stations for possible air play.

4. Start a Music Lovers' Club. Using lighter classics (Johann Strauss, Offenbach, Rossini overtures), offer weekly specials as an incentive for youngsters to collect classical records.

5. Donate surplus, outdated, or unsalable records to local institutions. An "advisory committee" is helpful to prevent too many demands for donations.

6. Hold a contest among local rock groups; record a session of the winner and press records. You may not sell a great many records, but your store name will become important to the largest group of record-buyers.

7. Sponsor a "Pickathon" in which amateur guitarists and banjo players compete to see who can play for the longest period of time. Scheduled over a weekend, when television news is low, this can result in ample coverage and even network exposure.

Photography Studios

1. Start a series of workshops with amateur photographers in the area. While the first, and perhaps the second, may have to be handled free, if there is "meat" in the sessions you can in short order start to charge and still benefit from the image.

2. Arrange with a bank or a savings and loan or other institution with which you do business to mount a display of your work.

3. If a local school has courses that involve photography, discuss guest lectures with the instructor. You'll have a better chance of success if you can show experimental work—polarization, multiple exposure, printing through textured screens, color intensification—which students and instructor alike will find innovative.

4. Sponsor an annual contest in which you specify the subject matter (medicine, sports, automobiles, architecture, craftsmanship). Gather as distinguished a group of judges as you can, and publicize the winners heavily.

Plumbing Operations

1. If you make emergency calls, capitalize on them. Announce an evening and weekend "hot line" service. (While there will be no commercial difference, the overtone of emergency availability is stronger.)

2. Enter a sculpture, made of pipe connections, in an art show or fair. Winning is less important than the attention your entry will bring and the sense of humor—considered rare for your business—it exemplifies.

3. Donate plumbing services to a worthy recipient— a family with financial difficulty or one that has been burned out, an orphanage, or a charity-supported school. While doing this ostentatiously is in bad taste, community service is always worthy.

4. Together with other tradesmen, form an Information Round Table that meets once a week at one or another of its members' premises or at a public building, with the public invited. The purpose is to give do-it-yourself instruction to homeowners—which inevitably results in business for you.

Printing Companies

1. Hold instructional sessions for high school and college classes in graphic arts, journalism, or advertising.

2. Distribute pads of "From the desk of . . ." forms to both key executives and secretaries of businesses, especially new ones opening or relocating near you. WARNING: Keep your own name off everything except a tasteful presentation letter or card.

3. Print bridge and gin-rummy score sheets; reprint rules of card games, backgammon, tennis, football, and soccer; and include some with every printing order. These should have your name imprinted as well. They'll result in multiple exposure of your name under favorable conditions.

4. Publish a booklet, "What Should Printing Cost?" This booklet should be distributed to all potential printing buyers in your area. It should leave the reader with a good idea of what his own printing job will cost. You'll have calls from people who otherwise would not deal with you. Discuss costs candidly. Include suggestions for saving money.

Real Estate Agencies

1. Many families not only do not object to a news release publicizing their purchase of a home; they welcome it. Ask at the time of the closing. If the release is submitted by you, you can control its content. Local papers tend to print all such items.

2. Establish intraoffice awards for salespeople: the Service Award, the Topper Award, the Good Neighbor Award. Issuance of the awards should be accompanied by a news story and photograph, sent to all local media.

3. Publish a pamphlet, "101 Things to Look for in Buying a Home." Content should be solid fact, not promotion for your agency. Give a copy to everyone with whom you do business and to every appropriate member of the press, and give multiple copies to commercial and industrial personnel departments.

4. Give an annual award at an art fair for the best painting of a building.

5. Activity in real estate organizations inevitably results in appointment or election to an office within those organizations. As an officer, you can become more of a spokesman for the real estate profession in your area.

Resorts

1. Standard news releases should be sent to hometown publications of all guests. With at least one out of three releases, include a photograph—a couple fishing, swimming, playing golf or tennis, or formally dressed at a dinner or social event.

2. Every few weeks, hold contests—some of which might require athletic prowess, some of which require none. Winners receive trophies. They'll not only keep them; they'll display them—constant image-builders for you.

3. Trade a weekend for a feature story. Call a specific

writer at a newspaper or magazine and give him or her an idea for a feature (world's toughest par-three golf hole, cooking for a big party every night, the psychology of resorts for the harried businessman, the importance of controlled relaxation, some scenic feature of your particular resort). Suggest that the writer come for a complimentary visit with spouse or companion. The more personal the invitation, the better your chance of success and ultimate coverage.

4. Using one of the many available television quiz show prize-placing specialists, arrange for a week's stay at your resort to be given as a prize on a major network show. The national exposure will delight local people who may be considering spending a vacation with you.

Restaurants

1. Restaurants are the most fertile feeding ground for gossip columnists. Invite them often, and submit "As heard in the *(Whatever)* Restaurant" anecdotes to them.

2. List on your menu the most exotic item you can imagine, perhaps nightingales' tongues or a dish that requires four hours to prepare. Arrange for someone (perhaps a theatrical personality whose press agent is groping for unusual coverage) to order the dish, well in advance. And invite the press and television to cover the meal.

3. For a week, sell coffee for five cents. Or for a day, celebrate an anniversary with prices that reflect the date you are observing. The anniversary need not be your own, if your restaurant is too new; it could be the twenty-fifth anniversary of your chef's entry into the world of haute cuisine.

4. If yours is an ethnic restaurant, many obvious ploys are at your disposal, from singing waiters to authentic costumes and background music. If the restaurant is not ethnic, you still can benefit from the offbeat: sitar music at specific hours, poetry reading during a "Happy Hour."

5. At specific hours, not during normal high-traffic

periods, invite anyone on hand to play your piano for a free drink. If the idea catches on, you will establish a popular tradition.

Savings and Loan Companies

1. Many theatrical events are poorly attended. Obtain, at a heavy discount, blocks of tickets and give them to your customers. Your community position will be enhanced.

2. Arrange with a fine arts center, art gallery, or school to mount displays of artists in your lobby. Photographs will show the artist setting up his display.

3. Sponsor contests. One large savings and loan association sponsored a "best beard" contest. The judge was a vintage television actress known only for her line for a shaving cream, "Take it off; take it all off." The event was covered by every broadcast and print medium in a sophisticated major market. Some columnists, even while calling it silly, gave it enormous press coverage.

4. Undoubtedly you and your associates are members of many organizations in your business. Arrange for a good speaker from your institution to be a speaker at business luncheons—and be sure that the speech is timely and bright.

5. While savings and loans regularly sponsor teams, you might find it possible to sponsor an entire league. What doesn't exist at the moment: a slow-pitch adult softball league? A tennis association? A backgammon tournament? By controlling the entire league, you must be a winner, especially in print.

6. Submit a news story to local media whenever rates change, or a new type of certificate of deposit becomes available, or a service is offered, or a key personnel appointment is made. While financial news often will be common to many institutions, remember that the one submitting the story is the one most likely to get coverage.

7. Issue news releases with comments on the housing

industry, automobile financing, and other areas in which you have a primary interest. You become spokesman for the industry.

Swimming Pool Contractors

1. Have regular swimming events—diving and racing—at your sample installation or showroom. In addition to events for age groups, plan father-son and mother-daughter races. In the diving competition, include "hot-dog" events that require no form. Be sure to have formal awards and trophies.

2. Negotiate with park districts or shopping centers for a week-long "swim-in," with swimming instruction at an above-ground pool. While this is a public service and should not appear overcommercialized, your name should be on the pool and literature should be available.

3. Discuss with each homeowner for whom you install a pool the issuance of a news story with photograph; the best of these will show children swimming in the new pool. (While some buyers will not want their new pool publicized, others will welcome the publicity. It doesn't hurt to ask.) WARN- ING: Be certain to have the head of the family sign a re- lease similar to the sample in the Appendix.

4. Depending on the type of pool, you might invite news media to watch as you "break the world's record" for speed in putting in (or, in the case of above-ground pools, putting up) a pool. Upon completion, claim the world's record and send a cable to publishers of the *Guinness Book of World Records,* with copy to all media.

5. Issue a news release whenever you refurbish or re- build a pool in a public location—park, hotel, motel, housing development, or apartment complex.

6. If possible, add nonstaining colors to water in a pool, fill the pool with milky water, or have champagne jets for a special event. These all are pressworthy and, if colorfully done, will attract television news crews.

Taxi Companies

1. On occasion (or regularly, if yours is an operation of fifty cabs or more), have a "Freebie Cab." This cab will take its riders to their destination at no charge, as the company's way of thanking the community.

2. Put together a tourist package—theatre or sports tickets, maps, and information—to be given to those picked up at airports, train stations, or bus stations. Even if an occasional packet goes to a local resident, the public relations value is substantial.

3. Prepare public service broadcast spots relative to traffic safety.

4. Issue awards for safe driving and years of service to deserving drivers. These awards should be made publicly (for example, at a luncheon to which the press is invited).

5. Have an annual Flash (or whatever) Taxi Day at a baseball or football game. Your own drivers will have free tickets; each driver will be permitted to sell tickets to cab riders at half the regular price. All ticket-holders will sit in a single section. Play-by-play broadcasters should be asked to acknowledge the event, and team members might visit the group before the game.

Theatres

1. Issue passes (usually valid Monday through Thursday to prevent interference with possible heavy weekend business) to groups that might identify with specific films. Passes to business neighbors will pay off in use of their parking lots and in goodwill and word-of-mouth publicity that might become important for a promotion in which yours is the pivotal business in the neighborhood.

2. For horror films, have lobby displays of caskets with corpses that occasionally sit up, live vampires, and nurses to help those who faint. You might also recruit a "fainting

corps" to scream and "pass out" during a specific scene during the first day or so the film is showing.

3. If yours is a community "live" theatre, it is imperative for you to develop a contact list for yourself or members of your cast. They should be interviewed by all media prior to the show's opening.

4. Maintain an active and complete reviewer list, and be certain that all logical reviewers, including representatives from school newspapers, are invited to see the show. Whenever you talk with reviewers for offbeat media, ask for copies of the reviews.

5. Submit news releases, with still photographs, to all media for each new attraction. Include a synopsis of the plot. For most motion pictures, prefabricated stories are available in the film's pressbook; for live attractions, have a photographer shoot during a dress rehearsal or stage special shots well in advance.

6. Initiate a local film festival. In addition to classic films (Bogart, Busby Berkeley) or "retrospectives" (Woody Allen), invite 16mm submissions from local area student or amateur film-makers. An additional category can be commercial films. Your panel of judges can be both distinguished and novel—newspaper columnists, local broadcast personalities, and perhaps a single "name" imported for the occasion to add an additional pressworthy dimension.

Travel Agents

1. Issue a monthly newsletter that describes travel bargains, exotic trips, and travel tips. Take pains to compile an active list, and be sure that people on that list know that you consider them above-average in travel sophistication. Request hundred-word mini-articles for the newsletter from individuals, who will become boosters of the newsletter and thus your agency.

2. Approach travel editors with suggested special fea-

tures to be written by you about vacation spots. Even if these are much-visited and much-written-about, you can offer a local angle: "What the Visitor from Ourtown Should Look for in London."

3. Call clubs and school groups to arrange for showings of travel films, with yourself on hand to answer questions. Prescreen the films to be sure they're interesting to the particular group.

4. Develop a speech: "How to Keep Your Foot out of Your Mouth in a Foreign Country." The title itself will assure some speaking engagements; additional speeches will depend on your own effectiveness.

5. Issue news releases about rate changes, new airline equipment, and schedule changes. Even though some of these may parallel news stories submitted by airlines and resorts themselves, your local angle will mean that your release has the edge for pressworthiness.

6. Form a travel club that meets monthly at your office, at your home, at the homes of members on a rotating basis, or in a hotel meeting room. You'll need some of your hard-core clients and friends to help start the club; they'll be the officers. At each meeting, travelers will show films and slides of places they've visited recently; you'll show a film (one of thousands available to you from airlines, governments, and resorts); and there'll be a light discussion of what's new in travel. The meetings themselves should be publicized by news releases to media, and on occasion a celebrity will agree to discuss a recent trip with the group. WARNING: Caution anyone showing films or slides to avoid scenes emphasizing that person's family instead of the location, or meetings will degenerate into a series of personal reminiscences that bore anyone but the presenter.

Truck Sales and Leasing Companies

1. Issue an annual Safe Driver Award to a local driver who has amassed half a million miles or more with no acci-

dents. The award should include a plaque and a public dinner, but not necessarily a cash gift.

2. Using the biggest truck you can get your hands on, enter a float in every parade. If your truck is big enough to hold something spectacular (another truck, a big band, all the members of a team, a number of youngsters riding bicycles), impact and image will be exceptional.

3. When new models are introduced, hold a formal showing, by invitation. Turn your showroom into a theatre and handle the truck showing the way you would handle the first showing of an expensive automobile.

4. Put together a talk on the history of trucking. Have visuals on hand—preferably slides made from photographs or from pictures in books. Offer the speech to club luncheons, to driver education classes, and to television and radio talk show producers.

Wrecking Companies

1. Invite the news media to cover the wrecking of a building. Be sure your workmen are on good behavior that day and that every safety measure is taken.

2. Work with a feature writer from a local newspaper on a story about strange items found when wrecking a building.

3. If you employ a wrecking ball, call the news director of a television station and enlist his partnership in a contest; the winner will get to operate the machine that swings the wrecking ball—every person's dream.

4. For some worthy project, publicly donate either a piece of the façade of a historic building or some building materials.

11 PR projects for specific "soft" businesses and ostensible nonbusinesses

Soft Businesses

The businesses and organizations for which public relations activities are suggested in this chapter differ from those described in chapter 10 in one important characteristic:

The public seldom thinks of them as businesses at all.

Therefore, in some cases the approach to self-aggrandizing must be oblique, even obscure, so that it is not evident that the individual, company, or group is actually doing what he is doing—slugging it out for coverage or recognition. Some professional associations discourage their members from overt public relations practices. Such cases have indeed been considered in the suggestions made in this chapter.

Architects

1. Establish an annual student award for innovative design. Students at all local colleges are eligible, and the panel of judges should include at least one faculty member from

each school. Entry forms should be structured, printed, and bound in pads.

2. Prepare a speech entitled "Trends in Building" or "What Your Home Will Look Like in the Year 2001." While professionalism prevents you from circularizing clubs and associations by mail, phone calls by a secretary or an associate will result in many speaking engagements.

3. Discuss with the local newspaper a weekly column on local architecture. Have three columns ready, at least one of which should discuss factually a local landmark; if possible, another should discuss any controversial public building. Avoid negative criticism of current work by a competitor; this type of subject can be handled with opposing direct quotations, reported by you as columnist.

4. Publicize any awards or recognitions you or your firm receives. If you regard direct submission of a news release as unethical, simply submit a fact sheet to the appropriate editor.

5. Submit articles to architectural publications and to engineering and/or technical publications about techniques and/or new methods you use. Include plenty of photographs and information aimed specifically at the readership of individual publications, and don't let rejections bother you. When an article is printed, send reprints to clients and to local news media.

Art Galleries

1. Become a true community institution by holding a block party. Arrange to have the street blocked off and run a continuous ribbon from inside exhibits to outside exhibits up and down the block. This can be a major news event locally and might be picked up by the wire services.

2. Establish an art appreciation class one evening a week. Whether you charge admission or not is determined by the caliber and reputation of those who lead the class. Or

use local artists as a panel. WARNING: Avoid dry and stodgy sessions that will kill off attendance. Be aware of the traditional as well as the contemporary.

3. Approach the nearest educational television station with an idea for a television show: "The Eye of the Beholder" or "Da Vinci to Dali." This should be a bright, highly visual show on art, neither pedantic nor technical. The station will listen, especially if you seem to have a self-contained package that isn't just your own commercial reflection.

4. Announce a contest for local artists. The winner, whose entry will be judged by as distinguished a panel of judges as you can muster, will have his works exhibited at the gallery.

5. Commission a work to memorialize some local event —the anniversary of a local historic happening, a building being erected or demolished, a group of famous people from your area, or a symbol of the community. The work, when completed, is to be presented to the community for permanent display at the city hall, county building, or library.

6. Send art materials to a dozen local (or national, if your contacts extend that far) celebrities—show business, sports, business, and politics. Invite each to paint something, explaining that the canvases will be exhibited and then auctioned off for charity. Those who submit paintings will see to it that their acolytes push up the bidding, and ample publicity plus enormous image-building for you will result.

Burglar Alarm Sales Operations

1. Work out a speech on "The Visitor You Don't Want" or "Mission: Impossible." Your speech will discuss ways in which homes and businesses can keep pace with the rising break-in rate. Offer it to associations and clubs, and demonstrate new electronic equipment at the same time.

2. In exchange for publicity, install an alarm system at any temporary installation that brings crowds—a fair, an

art show, a display of valuables. Be certain that your company name is displayed prominently, and demonstrate the capacity of the alarm system as frequently and publicly as possible.

3. Whenever a new device is brought to market, issue news stories relative to that device. If you are appointed to handle a system that is substantially different from others, call a news conference to demonstrate it.

4. Hold breakfast seminars for businessmen over a one-week period, by invitation only, and show your line. Such breakfasts are best held at a local hotel.

5. Offer a diamond ring to anyone who can reach that ring, located in the middle of a display room, without setting off the alarm. If the display is in a heavily trafficked area, you'll have wall-to-wall people as contestants try crawling, moving slowly, and using hooks and grapples to get at their prize.

Computer and Data Processing Sources

1. If you obtain the program to feed into a unit, challenge all local chess, checker, and tick-tack-toe experts to simultaneous matches. Prizes can be obtained from other businessmen who will share the publicity, or they can be dinners or theatre tickets. Be sure the press is invited, and "dress up" your unit with humorous human accouterments.

2. Offer a speech on "Your Second Brain" to business groups and clubs. Most businessmen, even those using computers, have only the haziest notion of how they work. If you avoid lapses into technical jargon, you'll have a popular and much-sought speech, because most computer experts *do* lapse into technical jargon.

3. Invite an entire advanced mathematics class of a local college to a speed match against a computer, on a problem the public will recognize—not an exotic, highly sophisticated one. The class can break itself into many teams or handle its approach "free-style"—you do nothing but punch

in the information.

4. As you make installations, ask the company or institution to approve your issuing a news release: it's to their benefit to be known as progressive in the use of equipment. Releases should be accompanied by photographs of company personnel using the equipment and quotations about the time and dollar savings anticipated.

Country Clubs

1. Invite specific groups—the chamber of commerce, a school faculty, civic clubs—for a day of golf. Memberships can result from familiarity.

2. Invite the best local tennis players or golfers to have an exhibition for members and guests. If you have a pro, he should be one of the foursome.

3. One day a year, open your facilities to the young people of the community. Have a "long drive" contest, by age-ranges, off the first tee; plan structured tennis lessons; and hold swimming events. Not only will community attitudes toward the club be positively affected, but members, because of increased awareness by the community, will have an additional source of pride in their memberships. WARNING: If the doors are thrown open and the day left unstructured, the event can backfire and physical damage can result. Control is the key to this promotion.

4. Whenever the club has an event—a golf, tennis, swimming, racquetball, or bridge tournament—send a news story to local media mentioning the names of winners. Many of these stories will be used, and each time a member's name appears in print you build internal as well as external public relations.

5. Negotiate for a weekly column on the sports pages by your golf or tennis pro. Many local papers would rather use a column from a local source than from a syndicated service.

Funeral Homes

1. Funeral directors have for a hundred years supplied chairs for parties, social events, community theatres, and civic functions. Maintain that tradition; your name on the chairs should be visible but not overly prominent, since public misunderstanding has made yours a delicate public relations problem.

2. Publish a free booklet that discusses death and funerals in logical, adult, literate, sympathetic, and (most important) non-self-aggrandizing terms. The booklet should be available openly, in quantities, to the public. A news story about its publication should be sent to local media—a low-key story, centering on the factual base of the booklet.

3. A speech, "The World's Most Misunderstood Profession," will make you a popular and sought-after speaker—provided the speech is presented with a sense of humor and is informative. Don't try to be too clever or tricky; remember that yours *is* a misunderstood profession.

4. Establish an annual award for the local resident who writes the best poem on a subject of humanity—life, aging, grief, happiness, hope. The winning poem invariably will attract press coverage; you also can negotiate for each year's winner to read the poem on a local television interview or news show.

Golf Courses

1. Offer golf instruction one morning a week during the season and one weekend hour (in the clubhouse or a public building) during the winter. Your students become your golfers, and their friends come with them.

2. Have a hole-in-one trophy ready for a winner. You may have two or three over a season, or you may have none. Since a hole-in-one is a golfer's finest hour, help him cele-

brate with the trophy, with free drinks for his foursome, and with a news story to media.

3. Publicize winners of every tournament and event held on your course. To milk the events properly, include every possible name, from semifinalists up.

4. One low-traffic morning a week, invite senior citizens for a free round of golf. Giving each player a golf ball will make the day memorable for the players.

5. Organize a regional tournament, a driving contest, a putting contest, a junior event, and any other possible golf event that will familiarize players with your course and result in news coverage.

6. If your course is in a northern state, have an annual snowbird tournament in which players use balls that you have painted day-glo red, tee off from snow mounds, and putt into snowmen. Suggestion: plan the event for a day in which major league sports have a light schedule; this will make possible more news coverage.

Hospitals

1. Issue a news release for each new piece of equipment or for each improvement. Over a relatively short period of time, you will build an image of a well-equipped hospital.

2. Publicize donations if yours is a nonprofit hospital. This will spur additional donations and build goodwill with existing donors. Emphasize the act of giving; unless a gift is unusually large, avoid specific dollar references, a practice that will keep some donors away. (See Chapter 8.)

3. Write profiles not only on key physicians but also on nurses and, even more important from a public relations viewpoint, on volunteers. These are human-interest stories that, properly written, will invariably achieve good coverage.

4. With each bill mailed out, enclose a small printed piece entitled "Your Hospital."

5. Once a year, publish an annual report that lists changes, improvements, and specific dollar information you want the community to have. This is your key public relations tool, and it is not inconceivable that it can be mailed to every home in the area during a fund-raising drive. Thus, it must have ample picture coverage. Copies should be presented publicly to the mayor, city council, governor, congressman and senators, and hospital chiefs of staff.

Interior Decorators

1. In this misunderstood profession, which has not achieved a great deal of promotable recognition for its practitioners, there is a real need for a weekly local newspaper column giving decorating hints for the home. The tips should make frequent references to "this part of the country" to make clear that geographical differences not only affect choice of decor but also make a national columnist inadvisable.

2. Author a paperback book on home decorating. You may wind up as the book's publisher, since you may not be a well enough known authority to persuade a commercial publisher to handle this book. But even if you publish it yourself, you can obtain distribution at local outlets with no difficulty, and the free copies you distribute will make you *the* authority in your area.

3. Issue an annual award for best decorating. There should be four categories: homes, condominiums, apartments, and business offices. If you've done your homework on this, the awards will be significant, the plaque you award will hang prominently, and the photographs will be used in local papers.

4. Sponsor a high school contest in which students are challenged to decorate a suite of rooms within a specific budget. They'll sketch, outline, and propose specifics. You and some associates will judge and award.

5. Together with other decorators, each participant can

decorate one room of a mansion, a large apartment, or a home. The press is invited to inspect, photograph, and interview.

Nursing Homes

1. Publish a monthly newsletter that includes news about your residents, and, equally important, their creative writing—poems, short stories, and news items. Poems, especially, should be encouraged, since they often will be reprinted by metropolitan media upon submission.

2. One night a week, invite an outside speaker to discuss current topics. Emphasize to each speaker that the subject should not be watered down just because the speech is in a nursing home. Take notes on the speeches and turn them into news releases.

3. Arrange with theatres, sports teams, and sponsors of special events to take a busload of your people to see the show. Once your publicity (which will also benefit those of whom you've asked the favor) begins to hit local media, you'll find the situation reversing itself, with showmen inviting your groups for their publicity value.

4. A touchy subject for speeches is "Growing Old Gracefully." But if your operating head is a genial, sympathetic type, this subject will gain many speaking engagements and perhaps a regular short broadcast commentary.

5. Write a pamphlet, "Grow Old Along with Me." Discuss how to care for the elderly, together with the economic and psychological considerations that enter into selecting a nursing home as opposed to care at home. Have an M.D. with whom you work append his byline for validity. Write a news release to local media, publicizing the availability of the pamphlet and suggesting that anyone wanting a free copy may phone or write for it.

Tennis Clubs

1. Your head pro should have a weekly newspaper column, and the only reason a local newspaper would pay a syndicate for a column by a touring pro instead of your player is that your pro's tips are useless or incoherent. Act as editor, and such a column about this increasingly popular sport will be pure gold for you.

2. Work with the public relations representatives of motion picture companies and touring theatre groups. When a show business personality who plays tennis arrives in town, it will be a natural mutual publicity item for him or her to play with or against the pro.

3. For a local charity, organize a pro-am tournament. Tennis is unlike golf in that handicaps are no help to a successful game, so be sure to group players according to ability.

4. Twice a year, invite the entire tennis-playing community to drop in to be "rated"—similar to getting a golf handicap. Players will be rated from 1 to 100 by your pro, who will judge the ability of each one. Soon your point system will become the standard for all players in your area, and you can expand the system to include rating cards, recognition for the most improved rating, and leagues that base the position of participants on how many points their ratings allow.

5. Even though yours may be a private club, cooperate with the local park system in holding regular tennis clinics. If you have a ball machine, bring it. It may recruit members for you.

6. Publicize club tournaments heavily. Get as many names as you can into your news stories. You can begin with the quarter-final rounds for all events—men's singles and doubles, women's singles and doubles, children's singles and doubles, and mixed doubles.

Ostensible Nonbusinesses

Artists

1. Submit "official" designs for local events—homecomings, chamber of commerce promotions, community anniversaries. Since those in charge of these events ordinarily do not think in terms of designs and logos, yours should be accepted with gratitude. Send a copy to the local news media.

2. When exhibiting, whether in a gallery or in an art fair, submit a news story to local media about the invitation to exhibit and the types of work you will display.

3. Conduct workshops for students. Three levels are possible, each highly promotable—"classic" art, new techniques, and commercial art. You can make money from the workshops and have press coverage as you do—what more could you ask for?

4. A friend should call media to suggest that someone from the "lively arts" department interview you because of some innovation you have introduced or some conclusion you have reached. Failing this, your bank may mount a show of your wares, and the bank's public relations department or counselor will submit the story.

5. If you're a teacher, plan an annual showing of your students' best work. Because the work is not yours but that of your students, you can unabashedly promote the event. The site is important. Use a shopping center, a theatre, a local government building, a financial institution, or a gallery—a student may have connections better than your own.

Associations

NOTE: Associations are so diverse and cover so many possible areas of professional, industrial, and civic activity that many worthwhile projects are better covered in Chapter

7. The suggestions here are for promotional activity generally useful on all levels.

1. Submit news stories with photographs to announce elections, installation of new officers, or any administrative change. Because of the vertical nature of associations, news stories should be sent to trade media as well as to local outlets.

2. Publicize all meetings on three separate levels: (a) the speakers and their topics, (b) the meeting itself and noteworthy business transacted, and (c) announcements made relative to a subsequent meeting.

3. If your group can be described as an association, it qualifies as the potential donor of an authoritative award. Awards should be standardized as certificates or plaques, and their issuance is newsworthy.

4. A newsletter has become mandatory for all active organizations. Adding circulation among logical outsiders will broaden the promotional base.

5. If you hold a meeting at a public location or at a hotel, work with the professional public relations people of the site to arrange newspaper and broadcast interviews of the speakers whose topics are most interesting to the general public.

6. If yours is an association within a geographical area, publish a map of the area showing members' locations; this can be distributed to all prospective clients or customers. If yours is regional or national rather than local, publish a directory listing member companies, officials' names, and pertinent information. If your directory is useful, you can sell space in its pages to cover production cost (and perhaps even to publish at a profit).

7. If yours is a chamber of commerce type of organization, offer free bus rides—on a double-decker or heavily decorated bus, or a trailer made up to be a trolley—to and from Dollar Day sales in shopping areas.

Auditoriums and Meeting Halls

1. If yours is a facility of any size, distribute inexpensively printed maps and instructions that show where the washrooms, water fountains, and exits are. Since crowd control is almost 100 percent public relations, you'll find that less confusion means greater orderliness.

2. Sternly worded signs turn people off. "Sorry—Fire Dept. Says We Can't Allow Smoking" is not only softer in tone than the mass-produced and impersonal "No Smoking," but it actually may work better.

3. On occasion, when you're not sold out, offer some free tickets to a children's or philanthropic group.

4. If you have shows or meetings that attract foreign-speaking ethnic audiences, prepare a small sheet of phrases that can either accompany the tickets or be available as people enter the lobby: "Where is the exit?"; "Can you show me where this seat is?" "Where is the washroom?"; "Sorry—Fire Dept. says we can't allow smoking."

5. Prepare and distribute news releases when newsworthy appointments, bookings, or events occur. WARNING: Don't prepare or distribute news releases when nothing has happened.

6. If you're hosting a celebrity or have an event that requires a press conference and for which there is no outside promoter, try to start on time so the media will love you, and try to end on time so your celebrity will love you.

Cemeteries

1. Do what you can to bring Memorial Day ceremonies to your grounds. You're already aware of the sensitive problems that can pertain to your business; any public activity must be extraordinarily dignified. A band might play "America the Beautiful" but not "Stars and Stripes Forever." Speak-

ers should not use the occasion to show off their rhetoric. Obviously, if you have a veterans' section, this is the place.

2. Establish a nondenominational meditation chapel in which people may sit quietly without disturbance. The chapel should be small, comfortable, and not funereal. Soft background music may help the mood. Understanding means understatement in such circumstances. Any touch of "schlock" means you're better off without the chapel.

3. Print maps of your grounds, showing directions, areas, and sections. With such maps, visitors will feel less lost and strange in cemetery surroundings.

4. Emphasize privacy. This includes screens around gravesites during a ceremony and cooperation with the family of a well-known person when they don't want the press underfoot. Thus, you become your clients' public relations man in a sense.

CPA Firms

1. Letters to the editors of local newspapers, commenting on government pronouncements that an accountant can penetrate, not only do not violate canons of ethics; they help position you as an authority.

2. If you teach a course at a local school or appear as a speaker or on a panel, send as a matter of course a picture of yourself with appropriate biographical information to the person charged with publicizing the event.

3. Establish a newsletter that is distributed to clients, prospective clients, and news media. The newsletter comments on recent tax court decisions, on changes in accounting procedures and tax structures, and on methods by which the businessman might improve his own understanding of bookkeeping.

4. Prepare a speech, "On Account of . . . ," and offer it to business/fraternal groups. Some, desperate for new subject matter, will agree to schedule you. Be certain that it's not a dull, dry, hackneyed speech with no new information; if it is, you're better off not giving it.

Credit Unions

1. Issue a newsletter to members, employer/management groups, financial institutions, and news media, with monthly commentary on best buys, credit terms, business trends, and local conditions. The credibility of the credit union will be enhanced and its position in the community strengthened.

2. Negotiate with a broadcast station for a weekly program—a commentary on the local business scene. A proper spokesman can make the program entertaining as well as informative.

3. When a member of the group retires or withdraws a huge amount of money, this might be the basis of a human interest news story that points up the benefits of belonging to the group.

4. Since credit unions usually are understood only by those who belong to them, offer yourself as a guest on radio and television talk shows to tell the public exactly what a credit union is and to answer any questions that might be asked by listeners or viewers.

Fraternal Organizations

1. Issue a news release for each meeting. Mention the speaker and his topic, important business transacted, and (as a mutual public relations move) the hotel, restaurant, or building in which the meeting took place. WARNING: Don't assume that because you're interested in intramural activities the local media will share that interest. Keep your releases newsy.

2. After each election, send news releases and photographs to all local media. If the president-elect is a professional, send a release to the appropriate professional publications as well.

3. Most fraternal organizations support charitable activities. These should be heavily publicized, and media invariably cooperate in this type of coverage. Any monies

turned over should be given publicly, with media notified.

4. When local members attend national conventions, prepare a news release listing the names of those who attended. Induction of new members is similarly worthy of coverage.

5. Issue awards, citations, and recognition for local activities: the (*Organization Name*) Award for the best float in the July Fourth parade, the best display for the high school homecoming, the best essay in a local contest, the outstanding local athlete or scholar. When a local government official retires, a plaque from the organization is a goodwill gesture that reflects on the giver as well as the recipient.

6. Ask for tickets for theatrical or sports events on off nights when a full house is not expected. Distribute these tickets to senior citizens or disadvantaged children.

Government Offices and Agencies

1. Arrange with a local television station (or, in a small community, a local radio station) for a weekly report to the people. Each week, a different department is responsible for presenting its function to the public, in a lively, informative, and entertaining way.

2. Working with a college political science department (or, if no college is at hand, a high school senior class), mount a continuing program of public sampling. Student volunteers will poll the community on local issues. Once a week, every several weeks, or monthly, announce the results of the poll at a news conference. WARNING: Avoid too controversial a subject—officials' salaries, school busing, political candidates—that may require an action that considered wisdom would reject.

3. Reinstitute the town meeting in which citizens can speak their minds. Properly handled, a town meeting can bring wire service and network television coverage (but if slapdash or half-prepared, it will degenerate into a worth-

less and poorly attended forum for publicity-seekers and demagogues).

4. Have an open house every three or six months. The public is invited to visit, discuss individual problems (the real reason for any visit to a government office), and have coffee and soft drinks. Humanizing the public servant is important in the Age of Skepticism.

5. Officials who are new in office, whether by appointment or by automatic sequential promotion, are worthy of news coverage. Issue releases with photographs.

Law Offices

1. Write letters to the editors of local newspapers, commenting on any event on which your comments might be pertinent. WARNING: Don't become known as a pedant or a crackpot.

2. On occasion, offer to represent a person or organization whose cause or whose financial circumstances normally would mean that the case could not be undertaken at all (or, if a criminal case, that a public defender would handle). In civil cases, choose those with a constitutional, human rights, or "underdog" overtone.

3. While seeking publicity is unprofessional as well as unethical, when you handle a case in which you as counsel are asked for comments, a news conference gives you better control than offhand comments fired from the hip outside the courtroom.

4. Discuss with the local newspaper a weekly column, "Your Legal Advisor." Such columns are available from syndicated sources, but a local source always is preferable.

5. When you represent one of the parties to a major transaction—a merger, buyout, or contract negotiation—ask as a matter of course whether news coverage is desired. If so, arrange the signing in your office. Personal recognition will result without the unpleasant overtone of publicity-seeking.

Musicians

1. Since music falls into three separate categories— classical, "popular," and specialty (country-western, rock, soul)—you can establish yourself as an authority in one or all of these through newspaper columns, reviews, or interviews or through similar commentaries or interviews on broadcast media. Submit these free-lance until your ability is recognized. Your position as a musician enables you to converse more easily with fellow musicians, and you can perhaps gain access where a reporter might not.

2. Commission a work of music. It might be a serious work, which you, together with others you recruit, will orchestrate and perform, or it might be a simple melody or a piece of music written to order (for a centennial, a local milestone or event, a sports team). Or you might have a contest limited to students. Publicize the winner and if no commercial recording is possible, record it privately and arrange for local stores to stock the recording.

3. To a local educational television station, suggest a series on local musicians, with yourself as coordinator (not "producer"—the station will want to reserve that title for a staff person).

4. Play at charitable events, hospitals, prisons, and schools. Don't wait to be asked; offer your services. If the AFM insists that you be paid, donate your fee.

5. Organize a group of musicians to present a music lovers' workshop at the library or recreation center. Much press coverage will result.

6. If you have a musical group that plays club dates and parties, publicize each appearance. Enough coverage will suggest to the public that you are *the* group to have.

Religious Groups and Churches

1. Ask local broadcast stations for time in which to present a program. Since most stations allocate a specific time

for such requests, you'll be put on the list. When your turn comes, don't present a sermon but, rather, a program that thoughtfully appeals to the station audience. Publicize the event as heavily as possible.

2. Issue a weekly news release covering the events of the week, including the topic of the sermon.

3. On a regular basis, "exchange" men of the cloth with other denominations. This not only promotes a reputation for progressive religion, but it also means ample community recognition and press coverage.

4. Publicize heavily major gifts and donations. (Be certain the givers agree; if they are undecided, persuade them.)

5. On major holidays, have your spiritual head issue a pronouncement. If he can think of one that is germane to world conditions, call a press conference for the event.

6. If no association of religious leaders exists in your community, organize one. Your representative will become the logical spokesman for the group, which can issue joint statements on local, national, and even international occurrences. There is little danger in condemning inhuman acts.

7. If your congregation has any strength in the community, organize a Day of Prayer. Invite business and government leaders to cooperate. The mayor will issue a proclamation, and perhaps the governor will cooperate in this non-controversial event. The reason might be world peace, a local disaster (fire, tornado, flood), or simply a generalized sense of timing.

8. Once a month, invite the philosophy department of a local college to appoint one of its members as "scholar-in-residence." On a Friday evening or Sunday morning, this academician will lead an informal, no-subject-taboo, nonsectarian, nonproselytizing discussion group. If the subject is well chosen and the participants enter into the spirit of the event, it will become locally famous. Press coverage is an obvious corollary. WARNING: With all activities, avoid cyn-

icism; approach any project with sincerity. And avoid pros-
elytizing, which will generate as many enemies as friends.

Schools and Colleges

1. Issue a news release for each individual who graduates. If yours is a residential school, the release should be sent
to that person's hometown news media, with a master release covering your local media.

2. Invite business leaders to underwrite seminars and
adult workshops. If your own faculty cooperates, these can
become important to the community; the cost to the sponsors
will not be heavy, and you can offer them a share of the
publicity.

3. Work with ethnic leaders in establishing scholarships
for minority groups. This is logical for both trade schools and
those offering general education.

4. If yours is a trade school, offer your students as
helpers where they can be used—for example, models for
charity fashion shows; students with building skills for a
burned-out home; secretarial help for other schools, government offices, or special events; drama students for Christmas
plays.

5. Schools are among the most logical presenters of
awards. Annually or semiannually, give awards for service
or recognition within your field of specialization, or, if yours
is a general institution, give an award for community service.

6. Offer public service programming to local broadcast
stations. Whether your series concerns English literature,
mathematics, vehicle driving, or fashion, you can structure
entertaining and worthwhile programs that will benefit the
station, the listeners, and you.

7. Stage something national—an award, the national
finals of some event (whether pie-eating or frisbee-throwing),
a national "day" of some sort.

8. Work with local merchants to have store windows
dedicated to your school. Homecoming is a natural (with stu-

dents painting store windows in wash-off paints), but gradua-
tion and the school's theme are equally possible if there is
no homecoming.

9. Once a month, issue a feature story about a different
faculty member.

10. The key to participation is involvement. Ask students to head committees and clubs. And (especially for public and high schools) ask parents to head committees and
clubs. Here are a few ways both students and parents can be
involved: a "Dad's Club," a homecoming committee, a parents' night, all social events that might require ushers and
crowd control (dances, athletic events, assemblies), parent-
teacher liaison, and fund-raising.

Veterinary Clinics

1. Offer a weekly newspaper column or radio program
on "Care of Your Pets"—or, if you have a sense of humor,
"How Your Pets Can Care for You." Failing that, offer yourself as interviewee at vacation time ("Your Pet's Vacation"),
seasonal change ("Your Dog's Fur Coat"), or back-to-school
("Send Rover to His Own First Grade").

2. Using national news as a cornerstone, send letters
to the editor whenever national news concerns animals—a
racehorse breaks a leg or a high government official buys or
loses a pet. Your comments often will be printed, and over
a relatively short period of time the media will begin to call
you for opinions and comments.

3. Publish a booklet, "How to Care for Your Pet in
(*Local Area*)." Even though the content may mirror that
published elsewhere, the local flavor makes yours preferable.
Put a one-dollar price on the booklet, but offer it free through
any outlets that sell pet food, plus your own waiting room.

4. If there is no local pet show, suggest to a logical
youth group such as Boy Scouts or Girl Scouts, or to the Jay-
cees, that one be organized. You, as judge, will be the focus
of activities.

12   ethics, professionalism, and the future

One of the problems besetting the entire field of public relations is that the people practicing it have yet to decide whether theirs is an art or a science.

Thus, public relations hangs midway between the soothsayer or medicine man (muttering mystic incantations and performing strange acts with nail-parings and typewriter) and the heavily—but too narrowly—educated doctor (prescribing remedies whose worth is tested through standardized means of research).

Advertising was in a similar position prior to World War II. "Seat-of-the-pants" experts not only did not have the benefit of formalized rules; they rejected such formalization because distilling their approach to a set of workable rules would have lessened their bargaining power. All of us know old-timers who still object to the influx of young people who have learned advertising and its rules—many of which coalesce after they have become obsolete—in an academic

cocoon rather than in the heated atmosphere of a cub copy-
writer's office.

As public relations moves on creaky, resisting wheels
out of the cave ("I'll get your name in the paper, baby!") and
into the board room ("Interpersonal relationships must be
psychologically correlated!"), we may be in limbo for the
rest of the twentieth century. Books such as this one cannot
provide a background of communications for a reader whose
preparation is too scanty: the beginning medical student cannot be told with safety, "Go perform a brain operation." But
public relations practitioners who object to transmission of
the existing rules are like doctors objecting to paramedics.
Sometimes a medical technician can take a blood sample and
do a better analysis than the doctor himself, who, thinking
on a more universal plane, has forgotten the cornerstone on
which his education was built.

Public relations has been an art more than a science; and
in this writer's opinion, if it loses its artistry, the world of
communications will suffer. Public relations will become auto-
mated, peopled by automatons following absolute and invari-
able rules, slowly settling into the gray sameness that has
shrouded other once-lively arts (such as music, painting, and
even the game of baseball). Dependence on predetermination
stifles creativity.

But it is equally dangerous to object to codification of
the aspects of public relations that can, by adding constant
professionalism, increase its acceptance by the public.

In its evolutionary state, public relations should remain
plastic, dependent on rules of procedure that will prevent the
confusion that would occur if phonograph records were produced by competitors at every conceivable speed or if rail-
roads decided to have differing track widths—but mindful
that mass communication depends on wit and imagination as
much as it does on rules.

To those who take public relations seriously, there is a
major advantage in accepting a set of rules of conduct and

method: both the charlatans and the masquerading amateurs will be eliminated from serious consideration by the profession and the media alike.

A horde of amateurs has invaded, smashing across the loosely guarded boundaries of professional public relations and storming into media palaces, demanding equal coverage as their just due. This invasion is not without merit. It forces those in the business, whose complacency is always a self-generated enemy, to pay more attention to their craft and its evolution.

On the other hand, the simple demand for attention is not what public relations is all about. And every indication is that in the next few years, brashness will become the only qualification necessary.

To suggest that public relations people be licensed is a violation of one's right to make an ass of himself. To suggest that in order to be considered for newspaper space, television time, or public appearance one needs the imprimatur of a licensed public relations professional would be parallel to the arrogant self-protection of the courtroom, where a judge will not consider an individual's probating a will or handling a simple petition without the appearance of a lawyer and where in many circumstances a lawyer appointed to handle a matter assigns another lawyer as his lawyer.

But those on the receiving end should indeed insist that they be given usable materials. An offer to rewrite a news release, to cover a useless news conference, or to honor a stupid stunt should be based only on (1) friendship or (2) recognition that the event is newsworthy but mishandled.

The Future

Will the Age of Electronics couple with the Age of Skepticism to create new methods of public relations implementation? Probably it will. Any new medium of communication becomes competitive with those already in existence and creates a new avenue for public relations action. When newspapers were the only medium, they were the only target. Magazines, radio, and television became added targets without eliminating newspapers.

Certainly something will come of the lame child, closed-circuit television. In-home facsimile-printing machines may be used primarily to reproduce the day's paper, but in peripheral time other promotional uses can be made of them. Direct mail is headed for eclipse as inefficient delivery and wildly increasing postal rates drive those who use this medium into cooperative mailings, lighter weight categories, and smaller samplings. But in years to come the mails may be a strong avenue for mass publicity, since except for one-to-one contact they are the most selective of media.

Mass conference telephone calls and videophones represent another potent future opportunity for public relations in the twenty-first century. These may become the successors to the news conference, which, I hope we have agreed, has been so abused that it may have been knocked groggy.

International public relations offers a pioneering opportunity to anyone willing to carve the trail across the world's jetways. Although many foreign governments hire high-powered and high-priced American public relations companies to represent them in this marketplace, only France, England, West Germany, the Netherlands, Sweden, and Japan have their own public relations industries.

The outsider has a difficult time establishing himself as a public relations authority in a foreign country. Despite the television satellites and the supersonic airplanes that have Americanized the world, many procedures stop at the border because other countries simply do not accept them. What one country accepts as part of normal marketing may be regarded as too timid, too brassy, or incomprehensible in another country.

Will accreditation enforce professionalism in years to come? This concept would seem attractive, but until the professionals themselves are more certain what "professionalism" means, it suggests more inbreeding and moving toward the center, with the individual squeezed out.

The Public Relations Society of America began a self-accrediting procedure in the early 1960s. As of this writing, substantially less than half the members are "accredited," and the organization itself seems to be splintered into special interest groups. Those who run public relations agencies have less in common with the public relations departments of giant corporations or government bureaus than they do with advertising agencies.

The Public Relations Society of America represents a membership opportunity of little value to the businessman who views public relations not in its philosophical sense but as another logical method of marketing what he has to sell. Similarly, local "publicity clubs" and "press clubs" tend to degenerate into in-groups rather than serving as instruments for improving the reputation or professionalism of those in the field.

Almost no academic courses in public relations appeared until the 1950s, when a sudden flood began. Many colleges now offer public relations courses both on the undergraduate level as part of a marketing degree and on the graduate level as part of a professional degree in mass communications.

Many colleges have found that their regular staff members are unable to teach public relations to those who want to know more about what to do than about the scholarly aspects of generalized corporate image campaigns. Thus, often the faculty for such courses is comprised of men and women in the field—a step toward practical education in public relations.

The Responsibility of the Persuader

Ultimately, reckless use of the channels of communication will lead to regulation. The only ways to avoid this disaster are to recognize what abuses may cause long-range damage and to educate those who run the channels of information to reject unfounded claims, unprovable statistics, and ads thinly disguised as news stories.

This is not easy to do. In real estate, travel, and amusement sections, newspapers may even depend on such material to fill their pages. And government, through both its bureaus and its elected officials, has been a principal abuser of the media.

The sometime user of public relations and publicity techniques is at the mercy of existing and competitive relationships when he attempts to operate ethically. Yet, using logic as a substitute for cunning, it is indeed possible to function just that way. That some of the giants in government, industry, and public relations itself continue to operate with profound cynicism, that editors and broadcast program departments are subject to pressure and payoff, that some public relations people are really "handshake and backslap experts" —these facts need not interfere with the evolutionary process at the grass-roots level.

Please don't misinterpret or confuse this comment. To suggest that the businessman should not use every claw and tooth to accomplish his public relations program would be worse than foolish; it would be wasteful, which is the longest step toward commercial suicide. The businessman should demand his just due from the media; he should promote the promotable and invent ways to make the unpromotable promotable; he should adapt for his own use the methods that have evolved in the practice of public relations. What he should *not* do is submit news stories that are outright lies; he should not fall into the muddy slough of rewritten advertisements as the sole basis of news stories.

And one other area of responsibility must be accepted by the businessman who has any public relations awareness: He must operate on behalf of the entire business community as well as his own enterprise.

Two communities are involved here. The first is the vertical community of *type of business*. Anyone in the hat business is in a position to damage everyone in the hat business; anyone who operates theatres is in a position to damage everyone who operates theatres; anyone who sells real estate is in a position to damage everyone who sells real estate.

This concept is easier to understand in terms of advertising than in terms of public relations. "They're a bunch of highbinders," or "I wouldn't trust any car dealer," or "You know what kind of people *they* are," stems more from advertising abuses than from prejudices. In terms of public relations, the bleeding may be internal. An editor may decide to refuse all handout material from an entire field because of abuses by a handful of its representatives; or, worse, the readers or viewers may reject as a matter of course all material they see on certain pages, view on certain programs, or hear on certain frequencies during specific newscasts or interviews.

Prevention of public rejection is implicit in the term "public relations." Yet it is characteristic of human shrewdness to believe that abuses which bring public skepticism into focus will not be damaging because they will be invisible within the total mass of information-cum-propaganda transmitted.

In addition to vertical responsibility, every businessman has a geographical community responsibility. If he operates his business within a city, he shares responsibility for civic pride and image. He should join local promotions enthusiastically even if he isn't the prime mover of such promotions. He should never lag when a shopping center or business section in which he is located tries to mount a campaign. He should try to boost and not knock. And he should be a doer, not a critic.

If some of these suggestions sound like the half-time

speech of a football coach whose team is behind 28-0, it is only because this writer is aware of the fragility of promotional thinking and the ease with which such plans can be yanked out by the roots and left at the roadside to die. "You can't do that!" is second only to "You shouldn't have done that!" as the most common tear-down by the malefactors of negative thinking.

In Conclusion

The methods of public relations aren't mystical. They don't involve phases of the moon, signs of the Zodiac, or pentagrams drawn on the floor.

If this book has disclosed useful techniques, use them!

If this book has exploded myths, don't be guided by those exploded myths!

And if this book has generated positive public relations thinking, don't let the motor die until you've done something!

The broad, dollar-green sea of public relations is warm and inviting. The bottom is smooth and sandy, and the rocks are far offshore. Dive in—the water's fine!

appendix I

Shown in the next pages are:

 ——a sample talent release developed to give the user full rights to a photograph or to film footage;

 ——examples of various types of news releases;

 ——examples of printed news release forms (no longer recommended);

 ——an example of a basic press kit developed by one company for local dealer use, through fill-in of names.

The reader can see that the format is fluid. Some news stories include a suggested headline treatment. Some have dropped the traditional "FOR IMMEDIATE RELEASE." Some are deliberately written to obscure their public relations origin.

All the examples of news releases reproduced here actually were printed in newspapers. In some cases, the names have been changed and the material retyped, but the basic substance is exactly as submitted.

How do your releases compare? If nothing else, the examples prove that this type of writing isn't difficult: it need only be workmanlike.

The Inverted Pyramid

One classic theory of news writing is based on the "inverted pyramid." This theory is sound, and one cannot err in following it: the story fires its biggest guns first, and each succeeding paragraph contains information of progressively lesser importance—an inverted pyramid of news.

A logical reason for this approach is that an editor, a copyreader, or someone in the composing room of a newspaper (or at the editing desk of a broadcast news department) who must shorten the story will have an easier time of it if all he need do is cut off the last paragraph or the last two paragraphs. Obviously, if this method is followed it is important that these paragraphs be less important. Hence the validity of the inverted pyramid.

On the other hand, the inverted pyramid leaves less opportunity for an unconventional approach. It is safe, in that it forces the writer to present his facts in organized order. It is unexciting, in that it is so widely used that it allows little room for individuality.

The structure of the inverted pyramid:

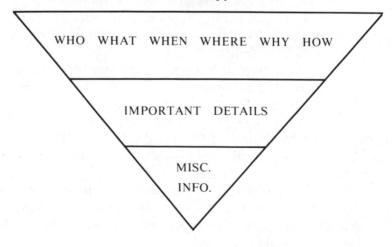

NOTE: Any information which might be considered advertising or "pitch" (i.e., prices, address, phone number, an invitation to buy or attend) should be put into the final paragraph so that an editor can excise these if he chooses, rather than killing the entire story.

Sample talent release

COMMUNICOMP
454 CENTRAL AVENUE
HIGHLAND PARK, ILLINOIS 60035

In consideration of good and valuable consideration, receipt of which is hereby acknowledged, I hereby give COMMUNICOMP and/or those acting under its permission and upon its authority, or those for whom it is acting, the absolute right and permission to copyright and/or use and/or publish, televise, or otherwise exhibit photographs, motion pictures, or recordings of me in which I may be included in whole or in part, or composite or distorted in character or form in conjunction with my own or a fictitious name, or reproduction thereof in color or otherwise made through any media at their studios, or elsewhere, for art, advertising, trade, or any other lawful purpose whatsoever, and hereby give permission to use verbal or written testimonials in any manner at any time or times desired by said Corporation.

I hereby waive any right that I may have to inspect and/or approve the finished product or advertising copy that may be used in connection therewith or the use to which it may be applied.

I hereby release, discharge, and agree to save harmless COMMUNICOMP and/or its successors and assigns and all persons acting under its permission and authority and those for whom it is acting from any liability by virtue of any blurring, distortion, alteration, optical illusion, or use in composite form, whether intentional or otherwise, that may occur or be produced in the taking of said photographs, motion pictures, or recordings, or in any processing tending toward the completion of the finished product, unless it can be shown that they and the publication thereof were maliciously caused, produced, and published solely for the purpose of subjecting me to ridicule, scandal, reproach, scorn, and indignity.

I hereby warrant that I am of full age and have every right to contract in my own name and for those minors for whom I am legal guardian in the above regard. I state further that I have read the above authorization and release, prior to its execution, and that I am fully familiar with the contents thereof.

_____

NAME

WITNESS:

_____

(FOR WHOM SIGNED, IF SIGNED BY GUARDIAN)

_____

DATE:

_____

_____

ADDRESS

PROJECT:

_____

Sample news release

The Scott Museum of Natural History
Centralia Road at Second Street
Phoenix, Arizona 62803
(902) 555-4576

Patricia Grant
Public Relations Counsel
news release (902) 555-2906

FOR IMMEDIATE RELEASE

3 DECEMBER 1976

19th Century Alaskan Eskimo Art
Exhibit Opens at Scott Museum of Natural History

In mid-afternoon, December 11, the Scott Museum of
Natural History opens the doors of Hall 27 to the public
with a stunning exhibit of 19th century Alaskan Eskimo
art.

[handwritten: Too much editorial viewpoint. "Puffery" should be replaced by a quote.]

The large exhibit (120 artifacts) includes ceremonial
and religious masks, household items, beautifully carved
weapons, hunting/whaling equipment, and engraved
objects such as buckets and bucket handles, pipes, snow
knives, trinket boxes and the like. These artifacts are
significant for two reasons: they are aesthetically
beautiful and they were created by people whose
language lacked the word "art". Hence, 19th century
Alaskan Eskimo art was intrinsic and intuitive—an aspect
of daily life which gave meaning to commonplace objects
which related Alaskan Eskimos to their demanding
environment.

The raw materials these people used were the
materials of their world: ivory (from the tusk of the
walrus), driftwood, bone, caribou antler and baleen—the
flexible strips inside the mouth of a bowhead whale
through which it filters its food. One of the reasons

—more—

19th century Alaskan Eskimo art — add one

whales were in such demand was that baleen was the celluloid of its time. For example, it was the source of "whalebone" stays used in women's corsets.

The artifacts in this exhibit are displayed in 8,000 square feet of exhibit hall. The hall is painted dark blue and hung with photomurals of Eskimos taken in the 19th century by Edward Curtis, the Mathew Brady of Eskimos and Indians. Background music of drums and Eskimo singers plays on a continuous loop tape.

Most of the artifacts were acquired by the Scott Museum in the 1890s during the first decade of its existence. They were brought together for this exhibit by Dr. William P. Jones, the Scott Museum's curator of North American Archaeology and Ethnology, so that we may focus on particular Eskimo skills and see what is easily overlooked: that these delightful objects related to all aspects of Eskimo life.

The exhibit hall is divided into three main areas:
1. Hunting and household equipment
2. Masks and ceremonial objects
3. Pictorial engravings on ivory, including prehistoric work, engraving styles that show the influence of 19th century contact with Europeans and Americans, and finally, pieces showing the influence of late 19th century and 20th century contacts with the outside world resulting in souvenir "art".

Folders available for 25¢ at the exhibit entrance serve as catalogs. When unfolded, the back face of each becomes a poster showing one of the masks in the exhibition.

###

Sample news release

News from: Knollwood Girl
Scout Council
2565 Second Avenue
Imperial, Kansas 55663
(999) 444-5956

Contact: Mark Saunders

FOR IMMEDIATE RELEASE

George S. Anderson of 4567 Sandalwood, Imperial, a *Who, What,*
professional photographer who finds time to lead a 12 *Where —*
year-old Scout Cadette troup, will serve as general *When, Where*
chairman for the Knollwood Girl Scout Council's 1976 *all in first*
Fund Drive. *sentence.*

The annual appeal, which will run Jan. 31 to Feb. 23,
will seek $22,500 to maintain the Council's growing
program in the north and northwest suburbs.

"This is the only time of year that the Girl Scouts
come to us as fathers and ask, 'Hey Dad, will you help?'"
Anderson told a cadre of fellow Scout fathers, known as *Too*
Neighborhood Enrollers, at a recent Fund Drive kickoff *obscure*
dinner held at Hope Presbyterian Church, Imperial. *a word.*
Under his direction, they are seeking to enroll parents of
more than 4,000 Knollwood Girl Scouts—as well as
friends in more than a dozen surrounding communities—
in this year's Fund Drive.

Contributions received are expected to constitute a
significant 13.8 per cent of the Knollwood Council's total
budget this year, along with funds from the Community
Chest and cookie sales.

###

Sample news release

Office of Information Services
LAKELAND COLLEGE
Lakeland, New York 78002
David I. Derwinski, Director
345-3600 ext. 676

LAKELAND COLLEGE
STUDENTS TAKE TELEVISION HISTORY TEST

Suggested headline treatment.

    Three Lakeland College Students will participate in
"The Great American History Test" to be broadcast on
WCCD-TV on Dec. 10 from 7 p.m. to 8 p.m.
    The students, all freshmen, are Donna Carson from
Merryville, NY, Roberta Lee Nielsen from Sperrytown, VA,
and Anthony Merkel from St. Paul, IL.
    The show, hosted by newscasters William Conners
and John Davis, will feature 100 area students competing
on two 50-member teams.
    The students will attempt to answer 25 questions
dealing with the past 200 years of American History. The
questions will be multiple choice as well as true and false
and will include pictures or songs from America's past.
    Audience participation will be highlighted as will
video taped appearances by government officials like
Illinois Senator Bert Johnson and New York Senator
Thomas Dodson.

###

*Note: This office has dropped
"For Immediate Release"*

Sample news release

Office of Information Services
LAKELAND COLLEGE
Lakeland, New York 78002
David I. Derwinski, Director
345-3600 ext. 676

76/446 *Internal code number.* *(handwritten)*

STAY SANE, LEARN TO RELATE
IN LAKELAND COLLEGE'S
CONTINUING ED COURSES

Optional suggested headline treatment. *(handwritten)*

You're late for dinner with the family and your
mother-in-law is coming. The cleaner has just ruined your
new raincoat. And you're being pressured to join a
committee that sounds like just so much busy work.

Note attempt to make story "brighter" by avoiding standard approach. *(handwritten)*

Suddenly, a semi overturns two miles ahead of you on
the expressway, and traffic will be tied up for hours. You
(check one) sleep _____, gnash your teeth _____, catch
up on your reading _____, participate in a spontaneous
dance-in with fellow motorists to the music of car radios
_____, decide to sign up for a mini-course at Lakeland
College.

The craziness of the contemporary scene and the
resulting complexity of personal relationships will be
discussed by Lakeland College professors in two evening
courses designed especially for adults beginning January 5.

One, entitled "How to be Sane in a Crazy World," will
be taught by David Krogsted, professor of psychology.
Previously offered in January '75, the course was so
popular that students strong-armed Krogsted to schedule
a follow-up during spring term.

According to Krogsted, the course is based on the
precepts of the 'anti-psychiatry' movement which caught
fire in this country during the 1960s. The anti-psychiatry
outlook can be summed up, he said, by two aphorisms:
Hi falutin'! *(handwritten)*
"Everybody in the world is crazy except you and me and
sometimes I wonder about you"; and "The only sane
response to living in a crazy world is to be insane."

—more—

Stay Sane, Learn to Relate   add one   76/446

Different definitions of sanity will be considered, as well as a wide variety of views about successful living in today's social, technological and cultural environment.

In philosophy professor John Lerner's "Closeness and Distance in Personal Life", the adult student will first become familiar with the one-to-one relationships experienced and described by such writers and thinkers as Jean-Paul Sartre, Martin Buber, Franz Kafka and Hannah Arendt. Later, they'll have the opportunity to share experiences of their own, and to re-examine them from a philosophical perspective.

Classes will meet once weekly from Jan. 5 through Feb. 16. They may be taken for credit or non-credit. Special tuition rates are available for students over 35 years of age.

For further information, contact Lisa Lowmann at Lakeland College, 676-4609, ext. 657.

—end—

This is a shift to imperative tense. Since paper may not print, it is last paragraph.

another acceptable way of ending a story

Sample news release

News about: From: Lang, Inc.
Vernon Symphony   675 Park Avenue
Orchestra   Vernon, Minn. 44359
                    (564) 565-2590

Contact: Sally Jenkins *Optional suggested headline.*

FOR IMMEDIATE RELEASE

Vernon Symphony Orchestra to Perform

The public is invited to hear the newly formed Vernon
Symphony Orchestra from 2 to 4 p.m., Feb. 8 at the
Vernon Recreation Center, 1850 Center Street.
Refreshments will be served.

Passive — not as strong as active tense.

The Vernon Symphony Orchestra, under the baton of
Herman Potter, is sponsored by the Park District of
Vernon. They will perform "Big Band" era music of the
1930s and 1940s. Sunday afternoon concerts, for
listening and dancing pleasure, are planned. The new
Symphony Orchestra is a total reformation of the former
Vernon Community Orchestra.

The call has gone out for musicians interested in
joining the orchestra. "All instruments are welcome," said
Monty Water, orchestra coordinator with the park district.
"Violins, saxophones, clarinets, flutes, bassoons,
trumpets, even guitars, mandolins, and washboards. Of
course, we'll need drums and at least 76 trombones.
Later, the orchestra will add vocalists and arrangers."

Nothing wrong with humor especially within an informative quote.

The Feb. 8 open house is to interest people in joining
and supporting the new orchestra.

Besides Potter and Water, newly appointed board
members are Susan James, board president, and Edward
Stevens, Vernon Symphony Orchestra librarian.

# # #

Sample news release

News about:
Sales Achievement at
Wesson and Keith, Inc.

More informative than just "Wesson and Keith"

From: Jerry Smith
Wesson and Keith, Inc.
2255 Center Street
La Mesa, Idaho 34340
(999) 676-4840

Example of how internal public relations can also be external public relations

FOR IMMEDIATE RELEASE

Wesson and Keith, Inc., Realtors, last week honored
16 sales employees and its No. One sales office for
outstanding accomplishments in 1975 at the firm's Sixth
Annual Awards and Recognition Breakfast.

They received W&K's No. One "Award of Excellence"
for their important contributions to the firm's success
during 1975, it was stated by Richard H. Blankenship,
executive vice president of the South Shore and
Southwest Suburban area real estate firm.

The Boise-Southland Area Office was named the Sales
Office of the Year.

The Southwest Suburban office rolled up an average
of $1 million per sales representative. It recorded total
sales of $10.8 million, a 34 per cent jump over 1974.

The top individual award went to Diane Black, sales
representative in the Springville Area Office, for setting
another new residential sales record.

# # #

Sample news release

News about: From: Northland Wallpaper Co.
Northland Wallpaper   7755 Shore Drive
Designers   Burnsville, Utah 99885
                                 (323) 222-9090

                      Contact: George Seeley

FOR IMMEDIATE RELEASE

Example of poor release: advertising, not news.

    Northland Wallpaper Unlimited has been in
Burnsville for twenty years. They offer two distinct plans
in interior decorating services.
    Also available at Northland Wallpaper is a complete
design service. Designers Martha Sunstrom Jones and
Dorothy Blaine have years of professional know-how in
the interior decorating field.
    Longtime Burnsville residents Betty Roberts and
Shirley Allslip complete the talented staff at Northland
Wallpaper Unlimited.

# # #

Sample news release

News about: From: The Jones Company
Santos' Hideaway   1414 Fourteenth Street
                    Springfield, Iowa 23451
                    (515) 555-2323

                Contact: Tom Jones

FOR IMMEDIATE RELEASE

[handwritten: First page of a publicity story. Compare with style of bylined, personalized story that follows.]

    There's a Greek Island in Springfield.
    So, if you don't have time to visit Greece this winter, restaurateurs Santos Christos and Charles Demetriou offer a one-meal alternative: Santos' Hideaway at 3206 North State Street, which lays claim to the title of the most unusual Greek restaurant in Springfield.
    The jaded dinnergoer who walks in expecting to find just another Greek restaurant may think he's mastered instant travel. Suddenly he has entered a terraced amphitheatre in sunny Greece, with soft cushions adorning booths that dot the tiers.
    "Anyone can open a restaurant," says co-owner Christos, whose first name is the basis for Santos' Hideaway. "What Charles and I decided to do is to make a visit to our restaurant a total sensory experience."
    Obviously, a total sensory experience involves more than food. To create the ambience, Christos and Demetriou hired young architect Socrates Prokas, who has the proper background: he was born in Greece and came to the United States about twelve years ago at age 18, to study architecture. A classicist, Prokas designed the terraced room to keep faith with the architecture of island villages that have changed little over the past three thousand years. The aisles lead down to the traditional center for all activities; lavish colors accent the white amphitheatre, and flowering plants complete the feeling of sunny outdoors.

# # #

Sample news release

Feature: Santos' Hideaway   500 words
by

You're sitting in a sun-drenched village in Greece,
sampling the fine wines, the exquisite Grecian cuisine,
and the happy entertainment and unmistakable
atmosphere of the Greek Islands.

Where are you? At Santos' Hideaway, 3206 North
State Street!

I'm not kidding. This is unlike any Greek restaurant
I've been in. And the story of how this unique village-
style restaurant came to be is both intriguing and
fascinating.

Two local entrepreneurs, Santos Christos and Charles
Demetriou, hired brilliant architect Socrates Prokas to
combine his nostalgia for his native Greece with the
architectural techniques he learned in the United States.
The result is stunningly effective.

It's a shock to walk into what appears from the
outside to be an ordinary building on the north edge of
Springfield and suddenly, as though a switch were
turned, be in the middle of a sunny terrace in Greece.
Socrates Prokas explains it this way: "Since eating and
sociability are so bound up in each other, the room
'where it happens' is designed in an amphitheatre shape.
In Greece this is considered the best architecture for the
bringing together of people. And the terraced room keeps
faith with the architecture of the little island villages that
build their town squares in the cozy dips and hollows
nature provides in its topography."

# # #

*Example of feature story: one writer only
can put a byline on the story as if it
were written by him or her.
Compare with other Santos' story.*

News release forms no longer recommended

FIVE
→ Pompous !

NEWS RELEASE

For Immediate Release

SCOTT CRAIG DOCUMENTARY PROFILES PLIGHT OF THE
"VICTIM"

Hour-Long Program to Highlight June Crime Month on
Channel 5

> "Starting with the Constitution, this country has
> shown a remarkable sensitivity to the rights of the
> accused. In contrast, there has been a remarkable
> indifference to the real tragic figure in crime . . . the
> one who suffers most . . . the victim."

Chicago, May 28—VICTIM, an hour-long documentary produced
and directed by Scott Craig, dramatically profiles the many
kinds of tragic problems experienced by victims of crime and
then explores a new plan of restitution currently being tested in
Minnesota. The program will be aired Sunday, June 9, 9-10 PM.

The broadcast is a special feature of WMAQ-TV's month-long
emphasis on crime, which is part of an annual joint
programming effort by the five NBC Owned Television Stations.
VICTIM was written by Bob Smith.

The Chicago SUN TIMES has called 1973 " . . the bloodiest
year in the city's history." A new record was set for murder. The
Police Department reported more than 12,000 serious assaults,
44,000 burglaries, and 1,605 rapes. For every one of these
crimes, there is a victim who suffered and who perhaps is still
suffering.

The first half of VICTIM focuses on eight such people in the
Chicago area. People who have been victims—whose lives have
been disrupted by an act of crime. These range from an
11-year-old hemophiliac who was beaten in his home by
burglars to the mother of a young man murdered in the family
laundry.

—more—

The second half of the program outlines an experimental plan designed to aid victims, which is currently being tested at the Minnesota State Prison in Stillwater. Under the Minnesota Restitution Program a convict is given the opportunity to "contract" with his victim to repay the losses incurred.

On-the-scene film shot inside the prison dramatically portrays a contract negotiation. Moreover, for the first time in the history of the state, Craig's crew is allowed to film an actual parole board hearing.

The broadcast also includes film footage of a number of convicts who have negotiated "contracts" and some who have completed them, as well as film of The Rev. Jerome Bangert, a "victim" who successfully contracted with a burglar in his home.

Others on the broadcast include Dave Fogel, Director of the Illinois State Crime Commission; Winston Moore, Warden of the Cook County Jail; Illinois Attorney General William Scott; Joe Pecoraro, President of the Chicago Patrolman's Association; and Harold Herrick, President of the Chicago Police Crime Fighters Association.

In addition to this broadcast, Channel 5 will present more than 40 other programs, features and editorials on the subject of crime during the month-long programming effort. This includes special programming on all public affairs series, NEWSFIVE broadcasts as well as editorials and public service messages.

Scott Craig, who is a producer of prime-time specials for WMAQ-TV, has won major awards from almost every key industry area. These include a regional Emmy from the National Academy of Television Arts & Sciences; ten Emmys from the Chicago Academy; and an Ohio State Award. With a Ph.D. from the University of Illinois, Craig also serves as a consultant and lecturer, the Department of Sociology, University of Chicago.

#####

Press contact: Ella G'Sell

News release forms no longer recommended

the **zebra**

news of interest from A. W. Zengeler

→ The reader's attention will be drawn to the format rather than to the message.

A. W. ZENGELER CLEANERS • 1010 TOWER ROAD • WINNETKA, ILLINOIS

Basic press kit

Three news stories each with a different slant. (handwritten)

𝒞𝑜𝑝𝑦 𝑓𝑟𝑜𝑚 **BUZZ BARTON & ASSOCIATES, INC.**

20 NORTH WACKER DRIVE, CHICAGO, ILLINOIS 60606   312-726-7101

CLIENT   J. W. Gibson Co.

MEDIA   p.r. kit rationale

Without an explanation, even a primitive press kit is of little value. Keep explanation brief and specific. (handwritten)

Dear J. W. Gibson Dealer:

The enclosed news releases are for <u>your</u> use, in <u>your</u> community, with <u>your</u> local newspapers and broadcast stations.

The releases are simple to follow. Insert your name and address where indicated, retype (double-spaced, please!), and submit to the appropriate editors.

Some of our dealers have done much more. For example, you might:

—arrange for an interview on a TV talk show, during which you rub icy hot into the shoulder or arm of the host to demonstrate how this type of product works;

—donate Gibson products to charities or telethons (we'll go 50/50 with you on such charitable activities);

—visit editors, leaving a sample with them for personal use, along with appropriate news releases.

A word of caution:

What you're doing is pure public relations. Too much public relations activities suffer from overcommercialism—news releases which are ads rather than news, demonstrations which are thinly-disguised sales "pitches", donations which aren't donations at all but rather an attempt to buy attention. Don't be greedy. Public relations and publicity are the frostings on the cake. You have superior products, which sell themselves. Your appointment as a dealer is <u>news</u>—sales features about our products are <u>advertising</u>.

Naturally, I'm personally much interested in your public relations activities. Keep me informed; I'd also appreciate receiving copies of any news stories that appear, and it will be my pleasure to send you a package of gift products as recognition for news stories that are used.

With every good wish,

Bryan Auer
President

Basic press kit

Copy from **BUZZ BARTON & ASSOCIATES, INC.**
20 NORTH WACKER DRIVE, CHICAGO, ILLINOIS 60606   312-726-7101

CLIENT	J. W. Gibson	SPACE
MEDIA	dealer public relations kit component	ISSUE

(NOTE TO DEALER: INSERT SPECIFIC INFORMATION
WHERE INDICATED)

FOR IMMEDIATE RELEASE

(NAME), of (ADDRESS), (CITY), has been appointed
an authorized dealer of Gibson Home Products of
Indianapolis.

The J. W. Gibson Company is the manufacturer of Icy
Hot, nationally known balm for arthritis, rheumatism, and
muscle stiffness, plus a number of other products used in
the home.

In appointing (NAME) as a dealer in this area, Bryan
Auer, Gibson president, stated, "It is a pleasure to have
an individual of (NAME'S) caliber representing Gibson.
His appointment means better service and more
personalized representation in the (NAME OF CITY)
area."

(NAME) has announced that Gibson products are in
inventory and available for immediate local delivery.
"Unlike many products today, Gibson products are
delivered directly to the customer's home or office. I invite
anyone to call me for a free sample and a copy of the
Gibson catalog," the new dealer said.

(NAME'S) business phone number is (NUMBER).

Basic press kit

Copy from **BUZZ BARTON & ASSOCIATES, INC.**

20 NORTH WACKER DRIVE, CHICAGO, ILLINOIS 60606   312-726-7101

CLIENT   J. W. Gibson   SPACE

MEDIA   dealer public relations kit component   ISSUE

(NOTE TO DEALER: INSERT SPECIFIC INFORMATION
WHERE INDICATED)

FOR IMMEDIATE RELEASE

    A major marketer of home products has announced a
new method of distribution for the (CITY) area.

    The J. W. Gibson Company of Indianapolis, whose
products have been nationally advertised for more than
fifty years, is adding local individual dealers to its
authorized network of representatives. According to
Bryan Auer, president of Gibson, "Many of our customers
are unable to shop during conventional store hours or are
disabled and unable to leave their homes. For this reason,
Gibson is appointing selected local individuals as dealers
who will service our customers directly in their homes or
offices."

    Gibson products include Icy Hot, one of the nation's
best selling balms for relief from arthritis, rheumatism,
and sore muscles; a complete line of shampoos, soaps,
and lotions; kitchen products such as dish detergents and
all-purpose cleaners; cosmetic items such as colognes,
hair sprays, and wrinkle removers; and general home
products such as insecticides and air fresheners.

    Among the first local dealers appointed by Gibson is
(NAME) of (ADDRESS). The new dealer has promised a
"grand opening" free gift to any prospective customer
who phones (NUMBER) for a copy of the Gibson home
products catalog.

Basic press kit

Copy from **BUZZ BARTON & ASSOCIATES, INC.**
20 NORTH WACKER DRIVE, CHICAGO, ILLINOIS 60606   312-726-7101

CLIENT	J. W. Gibson	SPACE
MEDIA	dealer public relations kit component	ISSUE

(NOTE TO DEALER: INSERT SPECIFIC INFORMATION
WHERE INDICATED)

FOR IMMEDIATE RELEASE

Remember the Fountain of Youth? This elusive
rejuvenator may be closer than you think.

(NAME), of (ADDRESS), local authorized dealer for
the J. W. Gibson Company, says that a Gibson product,
"Ten Years Younger", may just cause a user to look just
that way: ten years younger.

The Gibson Company has been manufacturing home
products for more than fifty years. "Ten Years Younger"
is their first attempt to peel years from someone's face.

"I don't know how it works," says (NAME), "but it
works. I have customers who swear by it, even after using
it for a week or less. They rub it into their faces, and
wrinkles start to disappear."

Obviously, (NAME) admits, "Ten Years Younger" isn't
a medical miracle. "If it were, we probably couldn't sell
it." Apparently it works by bringing moisture to starved
sub-dermal cells that, deprived of moisture, give one's
face that weathered, dry look that does indeed add years
to the appearance.

"I'm making no claims yet," says (NAME), "but I am
offering a money-back guarantee. So far no one has taken
me up on it."

(NAME) says (HE/SHE) will send information about
"Ten Years Younger" to any adult who phones
(NUMBER).

appendix II

So You Can't Write? So What?

You don't need writing skills to produce reasonably professional news releases.

All you need is this section of this book.

Following are sample news releases for most of the events and nonevents with whose publicizing you may become involved.

Here's how to use these samples:

1. Choose the release that most closely parallels your own project.

2. Change the names, dates, and locations so that the story is factually accurate.

3. Then cross-check the sequence listing to be sure you've included it all.

It might be that our sample will be a story on the park district schedule and your story will cover the library schedule;

it might be that our story is about a meeting at the Third Presbyterian Church and yours is a meeting of Hadassah; it might
be that our story is about the appointment of a new officer at a
bank and yours is about an executive appointment at a manufacturing plant. It's of no consequence: *you have here the
form—and you already know what the factual content is.*

Occasionally you won't need a news release. Someone will
say, "Send me a fact sheet."

There's no real form to a fact sheet. It simply contains all
the information about the occurrence. A sample fact sheet is
included in this group; all you need remember about a fact
sheet is:

1. Be sure to tell who, what, where, and when. If you also
tell why or how, don't let it read like an ad.

2. Put someone's name on the fact sheet as a contact
person, so that if an editor or broadcaster wants more ammunition he knows where to get it. An anonymous fact sheet suggests that there's a question of legitimacy.

Once you've used the samples, you're less likely to need
them again. And once you've disseminated a dozen releases,
you're one of the pros who could be writing samples, not reading them!

There's no point in, "Good Luck!" since luck isn't necessary. A better salutation: "Not to worry."

IMPORTANT

A note about headlines on news releases

As the text points out, some news releases have overlines
or headlines and some don't. This is an option for the writer.

In general, if your news story requires the reader to plow
through several paragraphs before he gets the point, indicate a
headline. If it doesn't, a headline isn't necessary.

If you use a headline, don't be tricky. Yours isn't the headline that will appear when the story runs; *it is simply a means of
letting an editor know quickly what the story is about.*

Typical headlines:
HER MAJESTY'S PANTRY IS NEW FISH & CHIPS
RESTAURANT
JONES PROMOTED TO VICE-PRESIDENT OF
ALLIED OIL CORP.
MUNICIPAL MUSEUM TO DISPLAY VAN GOGH
MASTERPIECE IN APRIL
JONES & MARTINDALE ACHIEVED NEW SALES
RECORD

If you're spectacularly clever, save your cleverness for negotiations with editors and broadcasters. Don't use your cleverness in a headline treatment: it may be resented, which means that the whole story will be rejected because of a personal reaction.

The sample releases herein do not employ a headline treatment. The releases you write might. Don't let it be a factor. Decide on the basis of immediate clarity of the first paragraph of the release itself.

Announcement of event

FOR IMMEDIATE RELEASE

The third annual Antiques Fair will be held at the Ravinia School Friday and Saturday, April 16 and 17.

According to Dorothy Jones, Ravinia P.T.A. president, more than 50 dealers will display their wares during the event. "This should be by far the biggest Antiques Fair we've ever had," said Ms. Jones. "Every dealer who participated last year plans to return, and we have more applications for exhibit space than we have room to accommodate."

Among the unusual antiques that will be on display are a Louis XIV mahogany dining table with inlaid ivory, valued at $20,000; a set of glassware which once graced the table of Queen Victoria of England; and a matched pair of rocking chairs that date from the American Revolution.

The Fair will be held in the school's gymnasium, from 10 AM to 9 PM each day. Admission is $1.00 for adults, 50 cents for children.

An innovation at this year's Antiques Fair will be an auction at which each participating dealer will contribute one item. Proceeds of the auction will be donated to the school fund. The auction, set for 7:30 PM Saturday, promises some unusual bargains and much excitement, said Ms. Jones.

#####

SEQUENCE:
1. Identification of event and date
2. Explanation by authorized individual
3. Unusual aspects, reason for someone to attend
4. Specifics of time and cost
5. Additional details

Business honor

FOR IMMEDIATE RELEASE

Jamesville resident Harold L. Marlowe, CLU, CPCU, has received the Prudential Insurance Company's Mid-America Trophy as the leading special agent in Wisconsin and Minnesota.

Marlowe ranked first in 1977 sales among some 310 special agents in the company's two-state Mid-America region to win the trophy, highest regional award in the category of Ordinary Insurance Agencies.

Nationally, Marlowe finished among the top 10 Prudential special agents, of a total of more than 4,000. His sales of Prudential insurance protection totalled nearly $6.5 million last year.

Associated with the company's Hennepin Agency, located in the Duluth Building, Jamesville, Marlowe was designated a chartered life underwriter in 1965 and a chartered property and casualty underwriter three years later. In addition to the CLU designation, the American College of Life Underwriters has awarded him CLU "Certificates" in Pension Planning and Personal Investments, Estate Planning, and Risk Management.

Marlowe previously was a winner of the company's Community Service Award, presented to him in 1972 for his outstanding contributions of time and talent to groups active in community betterment.

Marlowe and his wife Rachel live with their three children, Roger, 16, Marian, 13, and Julia, 11, on Lincoln Avenue in Jamesville.

#####

SEQUENCE:
1. Name of individual
2. Name of company
3. Name of award
4. Reason for award
5. Background of award
6. Professional background of recipient
7. Previous honors or awards
8. Family information

Business opening

<u>FOR IMMEDIATE RELEASE</u>

"Her Majesty's Pantry" is the new fish-and-chips restaurant at 500 Main Street.

Owned by Andy and Vickie Perry, the restaurant is decorated as a typical British pub. In addition to fish and chips, the restaurant features fried shrimp, ribs, and chicken.

Mr. and Mrs. Perry plan to keep their restaurant open from 11 AM to midnight weekdays, 11 AM to 2 AM Friday and Saturday. While at the present time no liquor is served, "Her Majesty's Pantry" has, according to its owners, the most complete stock of authentic British ales and beer in this area, including Guinness Stout on tap.

During the grand opening celebration, which will continue for the rest of March, each adult visiting the restaurant will be given a free mug of Stout. The restaurant has booths for dining, plus a "Limey Lunchcounter" for quick carryout service.

#####

SEQUENCE:
1. Name, address, and type of business
2. Ownership
3. Specifics of what business does
4. Any unique or new methods, products, or procedures
5. Benefits for customers or clients

Earnings report

<u>FOR IMMEDIATE RELEASE</u>

The Bank of Jonesville this week announced another strong growth period for the fiscal quarter ending March 31, 1978.

The bank has grown greatly in three areas, according to Jefferson T. Heil, president of the financial institution. Total deposits grew nearly $2.8 million, an increase of 11 percent over the first quarter of 1977; net income after taxes was up 26.8 percent; and the bank's lending area has grown to $13.9 million, an increase of almost 15 percent over the same period last year.

According to Mr. Heil, "We attribute this dramatic growth to two factors: our commitment to give complete banking service to a greater number of those in our community, and the response of the business community to our low-interest commercial loans."

As part of what it calls its pledge to offer more convenience to its depositors, the Bank of Jonesville this week extended its permanent Saturday hours. New hours during which the entire bank is open on Saturday are 9 AM to 3 PM; the drive-in windows will remain open until 6 PM Saturday.

#####

SEQUENCE:
1. Name of company
2. Identification of news
3. Specifics, including financial information
4. Quotation from principal officer
5. Additional news

Engagement

FOR IMMEDIATE RELEASE

Mr. & Mrs. Gerald A. Poston, of South Deere Drive, Libertyville, have announced the engagement of their daughter Patricia to Murray K. Deane of Boston, Massachusetts.

A June wedding is planned.

The couple met at Boston University, where Ms. Poston is a senior in business administration and Mr. Deane is in the graduate school of mass communications. After the wedding, the couple plan an extended trip, following which they will reside in the Boston area while Mr. Deane studies toward a doctorate in mass communications.

SEQUENCE:
1. Name and address of parents of bride
2. Name of engaged couple
3. Date of wedding
4. Background information
5. Future plans

Executive appointment, previously unaffiliated

FOR IMMEDIATE RELEASE

John W. Jones is the new vice-president of Brown & Co., according to Robert J. Brown, president of the local department store, effective April 1, 1977.

Jones is well known in department store administration, having spent the past six years as a marketing and operations executive with a major retail chain located in Columbus, Ohio.

"It's a pleasure for us to have a man of Mr. Jones' caliber on our management staff," commented Mr. Brown. "In addition to responsibilities in merchandising, he will be in charge of personnel."

A native of Illyria, Ohio, Jones attended Illyria College, graduating with honors in 1970. He is married to the former Audrey White. The couple have two sons, James, 9, and Robert, 7.

#####

SEQUENCE:
1. Name of individual
2. Name of authority issuing statement
3. Previous business history—it may be inadvisable to mention specific company by name
4. Direct quotation by authority
5. Personal history
6. Personal family information—no address if individual has not yet relocated

Exhibit

FOR IMMEDIATE RELEASE

The Plainton Museum of Art, which this year is celebrating its fiftieth anniversary, will exhibit rare lithographs by the modern master Marc Chagall during the month of November.

According to Museum Director Roy Sherman, the exhibition, titled "Chagall's Colorful World," has been made possible because of the philanthropy of Mr. and Mrs. Harris Brown, local art patrons who have loaned three lithographs and two Chagall originals, each valued at more than $50,000, for this exhibition. Other Chagall lithographs have been obtained for exhibition from several other museums, some as far away as Los Angeles.

Born in 1887 in Russia, Chagall generally is regarded as French, having moved to France permanently in 1910. His paintings are instantly recognizable for their dreamlike quality, their bright colors, and recurring themes such as roosters and rooftop violinists.

"I suggest that every resident of Plainton visit this Chagall exhibit," commented Sherman. "With works of art being dispersed, held tightly by museums, and hidden by collectors, and with insurance rates becoming prohibitive, there may never be another display such as this."

#####

SEQUENCE:
1. Name of institution
2. Name of event
3. Explanation of how exhibition came to be
4. Biographical information about artist, or specifics of displays
5. Direct quotation urging attendance and giving reason

Fair or show

FOR IMMEDIATE RELEASE

The 15th annual Country Peddler's Antique Show and Sale will be held on the Lincoln Fairgrounds, Danielsburg, October 9, 10, and 11.

According to Otto Knight, managing director of the fair, more than 50 dealers will exhibit fine furniture, art glass, pottery, silver, primitives, jewelry, depression glass, and other unusual collectibles. Attendance is expected to exceed that of last year's fair, which attracted more than 5,000 visitors.

"We think this will be the biggest and best-attended fair we've ever had," said Knight. "Nearly two million dollars' worth of antiques will be on display, representing the best antique dealers in this entire area."

New this year is "Collectors' Row," which will show such contemporary collectibles as beer cans, comic books, and collector's plates.

#####

SEQUENCE:
1. Name of event
2. Location and date
3. Specific details, validated by authority
4. Direct quotation by authority
5. Innovations

Fund-raising activity

<u>FOR IMMEDIATE RELEASE</u>

The League of Women Voters of Oak River will hold a garage sale Friday and Saturday, May 7 and 8, from 9 AM to 5 PM at the Lincoln School, 1000 Lincoln Avenue South.

Useful items from bicycles to microwave ovens, donated by the League's members, will be offered for sale. A special section will offer more than 1,000 books.

Proceeds from the event will be used to help the League continue its role of furthering political responsibility and community action, plus providing service to voters through voter registration drives, presentation of candidates, and issuance of voter guides.

The League also maintains a Speakers Bureau and holds regular workshops for its members and friends. This sale is the only fund-raising event held by the League this year.

#####

SEQUENCE:
1. Name of organization
2. Name of event
3. Dates and times of day
4. Location
5. Specifics of activity and offers
6. Explanation of organization activity
7. Justification for event

Fund-raising event

FOR IMMEDIATE RELEASE

Mary Miller will star in a special benefit performance of the hit comedy, "Under Papa's Picture," at the Schubert Theatre in Johnson City, Thursday, September 13 at 8 PM.

Proceeds of the performance will go toward the funding of a sheltered residence for employed mentally damaged young adults.

Tickets for the performance are $16 each and can be obtained either from the theatre box office, by calling the Johnson City Association for the Retarded at 555-6543, or by contacting Judith Anne Sloan, benefit chairman, at 555-5432.

The Association sponsors both schooling and training centers for mentally handicapped adults. It is the only organization, public or private, dedicated to this work in southeast Iowa.

According to Association president Patricia James, the new residence is designed to provide semi-independent lifestyle for young adults who have gained competence through the Association's educational and vocational programs. "We're grateful not only to Ms. Miller but to the entire management and staff of the Schubert Theatre," said Ms. James. "It's always gratifying to learn that others recognize the need for help to establish and maintain circumstances in which those with mental disabilities can build normal lives for themselves."

Mary Miller has promised to visit with the audience after the performance and to give her famous monolog, "Walking the Dog."

#####

SEQUENCE:
1. Name of event
2. What the project is
3. Specifics of price and availability
4. Validation of organization's credentials
5. Quotation from officer of organization
6. Additional information to heighten interest

Ostensible public service

FOR IMMEDIATE RELEASE

Ride before you buy.

That's the advice of a leading Burnside bicycle expert, Jerry Mahan, who heads Cycle-Rama, on Central Avenue.

"Every day, we hear of someone who has bought a bike that's too big, too small, too slow, or too fast," Mahan explains. "Most kids will say automatically, 'I want a 10-speed bike.' As often as not, they want the 10-speed because that's what the racers ride, not because it's what they should have."

One major problem, according to Mahan, is the parent who wants the child to have a bigger or more complicated bicycle than the child should have. The result can be dangerous, especially for the inexperienced cyclist.

"My suggestion is that bicycles be treated like automobiles," comments the cycle expert. "Don't surprise a boy or a girl with a bike. Have him or her ride it."

Mahan points out that a child's feet should touch the ground when fully extended. If they don't the bicycle is too big. And no youngster, he says, should have a 10-speed as the first bicycle.

Cycle-Rama, at 225 Central Avenue, is the local dealer for Raleigh, Schwinn, and Fuji cycles. The store is open daily from 9 AM to 6 PM.

#####

SEQUENCE:
1. Public service message
2. Source/authority
3. Direct quotation explaining and expanding on message
4. Specific advice based on message
5. Ancillary information
6. Commercial information

Personal honor

<u>FOR IMMEDIATE RELEASE</u>

Michael A. Jones, 555 Bartlett Road, Jonesville, has attained the degree of Master Mason at A. O. Fay Masonic Lodge on April 20.

Stephen Zimmer of Pricedale was Jones' sponsor and instructor of Masonic rituals which culminated in his elevation to the degree of Master Mason.

#####

SEQUENCE:
1. Name and address of individual honored
2. Name of honor or award
3. Background information

Product introduction

FOR IMMEDIATE RELEASE

First local look at the 1978 Fords will be 7 PM
Monday, September 19 at the Brown Motor Company,
1111 Broadway, Denton, according to Robert J. Brown,
president of the local dealership.

Brown, a Ford dealer for 27 years, has promised some
styling and engineering surprises for the 1978 models.
"The Granada and Pinto have been completely
redesigned," he comments. "The Maverick has a
completely new engine that will deliver far better mileage
than ever before. And the LTD has a new interior
treatment to match some of the highest-priced luxury
cars."

To mark the introduction, Brown Motor Company will
have some surprises of its own the evening of September
19. Champagne punch and hors d'oeuvres will be served
to visitors at the showroom. Each adult visitor will receive
a gift. Music and entertainment will be provided, and
special "Kiddie Ford" rides for the youngsters are
intended to keep them happily occupied while their
parents inspect the new models.

"We'll stay open Monday night as long as visitors
want us to," said Mr. Brown. Regular showroom hours for
Brown Motor Company are 10 AM to 9 PM Monday
through Friday, and 10 AM to 5 PM Saturday and
Sunday.

#####

SEQUENCE:
1. Name of event
2. Date
3. Location
4. Name of authority issuing statement
5. Specifics, with puffery in quotes
6. Additional details of what might be expected

Professional organization membership

<u>FOR IMMEDIATE RELEASE</u>

Two realtors and 12 realtor-associates were inducted into the Stockton-South Shore Board of Realtors at a members' dinner meeting Monday, February 6, in the Sheraton-South Shore Inn in Stockton.

Realtors are Joseph T. Case of Case & Associates and Malon T. Hand of Stockton Realty Company.

Realtor-associates include Charles Levine and Harmon Stone, A.B.C. Realty; Virginia Larson and Mary Jacobs, Century Realty; Jeffrey Young, Clark Realty; Gloria McManus and Myrna White, Delworth and Dimity; Clark Sutherland and Loren Horner, Home Exchangers, Inc.; R. L. Clermont and Marshall Thompson, Rich County Realty; and Marcia Wade, Velasco Brothers, Inc.

#####

SEQUENCE:
1. Identification of event
2. Date and place
3. Individual names of member-inductees, alphabetically by company

Promotion from within

FOR IMMEDIATE RELEASE

John W. Jones has been elected vice-president of Brown & Co., according to Robert J. Brown, president of the local department store.

Jones has been with Brown & Co. for the past six years as assistant vice-president in charge of operations. "It's a pleasure to acknowledge the effectiveness of John Jones by this promotion," said Mr. Brown. "In his new position, Mr. Jones will be responsible for both merchandising and personnel."

A native of Illyria, Ohio, Jones attended Illyria College, graduating with honors in 1970. Prior to joining Brown & Co., he held a position with the operations division of Sears, Roebuck & Co. Together with his wife Audrey and their two sons, James, 9, and Robert, 7, they live in the Lakeview area of Cincinnati.

#####

SEQUENCE:
1. Name of individual
2. Name of authority issuing statement
3. Previous relationship with company
4. Direct quotation from authority
5. Personal history
6. Personal family information

Public lecture or speech

FOR IMMEDIATE RELEASE

The Streeterville YWCA will sponsor a lecture-discussion on UFOs Tuesday, December 4, from 7:30 to 9:30 PM in the auditorium of the YWCA, 700 Third Street.

John Brown, associate director of the Astro-Science Institute, will lead the discussion and show rare photographs which purport to be of extraterrestrial visitors. Brown is an internationally-recognized authority on UFOs who has done research in astronomy and UFOs at the Northwestern University Center for UFO Study.

Brown also is the author of the monograph, "UFOs—Fact or Fancy," and is visiting professor of astronomy at Streeterville University.

Admission for the session is $1.50 for YWCA members, $2.50 for nonmembers.

#####

SEQUENCE:
1. Name of organization
2. Name of event
3. Date and time of day
4. Location
5. Identification and credentials of speaker
6. Teaser, if any, to add reader interest
7. Cost or qualification to attend

Record sales volume

FOR IMMEDIATE RELEASE

Jones and Martindale, Inc., realtors, has set an all-time monthly sales record, with sales of $2.3 million during March.

The sales mark topped the previous monthly high, set in April of 1976, it was announced by Jeremy T. Martindale, executive vice-president and general manager of residential sales.

In the first three months of this year, the Jacksonburg real estate firm also recorded the best first quarter in its history. First quarter sales totalled $5.8 million, up nearly $1 million from the same period of last year.

The Broad Avenue office led all four offices in March, with $865,000 in sales. The Jackson Building office had more than $500,000 in sales.

"We look forward to an even stronger second quarter," said Mr. Martindale. "The residential housing market never has seemed stronger, and the opening of our new suburban office in Jackson Heights should contribute significantly to total sales."

#####

SEQUENCE:
1. Name of company
2. Specifics of achievement, including name of individual as source
3. Comparison with previous activity
4. Additional background
5. Comments by corporate officer

Religious meeting

FOR IMMEDIATE RELEASE

Rev. and Mrs. Hanford S. Sloan, missionaries with the United Gospel Mission (UGM) to Zaire, Africa, will speak at the United Church of Christ, First Avenue and Lombard Street, Blackburn, Wednesday, October 8, at 7:30 PM.

UGM is an interdenominational sending agency with nearly 300 missionaries and homeland staff in 16 countries plus the United States, and headquartered in Jasper, Kansas.

Rev. and Mrs. Sloan both are graduates of the Kinnard College of Divine Science, Kinnard, Nebraska. Each also holds a master of arts degree from Columbus College, Columbus, Illinois.

With their special interest in Bible teaching, the Sloans promoted and literally built the Bible School in Angawa, a village in Zaire. They plan to show slides and motion pictures illustrating their unusual experiences in Africa.

Tea and refreshments are planned following the meeting Wednesday evening.

#####

SEQUENCE:
1. Names of principals
2. Identification of affiliation
3. Name of event
4. Explanation of terms and names
5. Background of individuals
6. Specifics of meeting
7. Additional details

Scholastic honor

FOR IMMEDIATE RELEASE

    Eloise Forbes has been named to the Dean's List at Knollwood University, Knollwood, Indiana.

    Ms. Forbes, daughter of Mr. and Mrs. William Forbes of Fowler Avenue, Springfield, is a junior in the College of Liberal Arts at Knollwood.

    The Dean's List is an honor limited to those who have shown outstanding scholastic achievement and who have shown leadership in campus activities. According to Dr. Harmon Charles, dean of students, "Ms. Forbes has shown an enviable record at Knollwood, not only as a student but as a leader. Being named to the Dean's List is a symbol of her academic accomplishments."

#####

SEQUENCE:
1. Name of individual
2. Honor
3. Identification of individual and family
4. Explanation of honor
5. Quotation by authority

Speech

FOR IMMEDIATE RELEASE

"Watch Those Minor Contracts!"
That's the subject of the talk scheduled for the
Northview Lions Club luncheon Tuesday, October 11.
Arthur W. Johnson, Northview attorney who specializes in
contract law, will be the featured speaker.

According to Wilbur Brown, program chairman of the
club, "Every businessman should be interested in this
topic, which isn't what one at first might think it is. It has
to do with the dangers someone can encounter when he
enters into a contract with someone who isn't of legal age.
And Mr. Johnson is one of the most entertaining speakers
we've ever been privileged to hear."

The Northview Lions Club meets at noon Tuesdays at
the Northview Hotel. Ralph Stern, head of Stern Brothers
Clothiers, is president of the local chapter.

#####

SEQUENCE:
1. Eye-catcher
2. Explanation of event
3. Comment by authority
4. Background specifics

Sports event

FOR IMMEDIATE RELEASE

The Northville Lions Club softball team defeated a stubborn Mike's Pizza squad 16-14 in a 16-inch league game Tuesday evening.

Leading the Lions team was Hank O'Neill, who collected four hits including the game's only home run. For the losers, Tony Kozlowski had three hits, one of which was a triple that tied the game in the fifth inning.

The Lions, with a 10-4 record, now are second in the league, behind Gaynor Chevrolet, which has won 12 and lost 2. Other teams in the league, in addition to Mike's Pizza, are The Optimists, Burns Lincoln-Mercury, Nickels Industries, Northville Bottling Co., and Northville Power & Light. The league is sponsored by the Northville Park District. Adults over 30 who are interested in playing on one of the teams are invited to contact Park District Superintendent Jim Sullivan at 555-7654.

#####

SEQUENCE:
1. Identification of event and results
2. Names of outstanding players
3. Team or league information
4. Background (optional depending on local situation and length of season)

Stage presentation

FOR IMMEDIATE RELEASE

The Fine Arts Department of Central Park High
School will present its spring musical, *Carousel* by
Rodgers and Hammerstein, May 16 and 17 at 8 PM in the
high school auditorium.

Carousel is based on the famous play *Liliom* by
Ferenc Molnar, about a carousel barker, Billy Bigelow,
who falls in love with the gentle Julie, a worker at a local
mill. The musical features such favorite Rodgers and
Hammerstein songs as, "June Is Bustin' Out All Over," "If
I Loved You," and "When You Walk Through a Storm."

In the local production, Billy Bigelow will be played
by Mark Johnson, son of Mr. & Mrs. Louis Johnson of
Margot Avenue; Julie will be played by Marie Green,
daughter of Mrs. Louise Green of Eighteenth Street and
the late James Green.

The production, directed by Elaine Schneider, head of
the CPHS Drama Department, includes on its staff Henry
L. Smythe, musical conductor; Katherine Lord,
choreographer; and Ellyn Forbes, costume director. The
opening scene, filmed on the carousel at Centralia
Amusement Park, was photographed by Richard Harris.
Sets were designed by Tom Riddle.

Approximately 200 students are involved in the cast,
chorus, orchestra, and crew. Admission for the
performances is $1.25 for students, $2.50 for adults.

#####

SEQUENCE:
1. Name of organization
2. Name of production
3. Date, time, and place
4. Synopsis of storyline
5. Names of featured players
6. Production credits
7. Admission price

Straight commercial puffery

FOR IMMEDIATE RELEASE

Jackson Bros. Greenhouse this week is celebrating its 28th anniversary of doing business in Madisonville.

Founded by Mark and Richard Jackson in 1949, the greenhouse, one of the largest commercial horticulture companies in the area, is the home of the famous "Squatter's Oak," the mammoth oak tree which was on the property long before the greenhouse was established and which now grows inside the south end of the greenhouse, its huge branches towering above the roof. "We built our greenhouse around that tree," said co-founder Mark Jackson, "and we plan to be here as long as the tree is here."

Dendrochronologists—specialists who estimate the age of trees—have placed the Squatter's Oak at more than a hundred years of age. "That oak was here long before the town was here," commented Richard Jackson.

The original greenhouse is only one of three greenhouses that Jackson Bros. have erected since opening their doors 28 years ago. In it are literally thousands of geraniums in full bloom. Richard Jackson indicated that the "Red Irene" geranium is the most popular flower the greenhouse grows. "We start them in December and January," he explained, "and by Mother's Day this part of the greenhouse is the most colorful spot in town." Also in the main greenhouse are ivy, petunias, many types of ferns, and other popular flowers.

The "Red Greenhouse," so called because its steel struts are painted bright red, contains annuals such as zinnias, petunias, and snapdragons. The newest greenhouse, which has automatic controls for both heat and humidity, is the source for exotic and out-of-season fruits and vegetables. "We had a customer last week who bought every melon we had that was anywhere near ripe," said Mark Jackson. "It was for a party, and he wanted ripe melons. We had 'em."

Jackson Bros. Greenhouse is located on Third Street, at the eastern end of town just beyond Morris Avenue.

#####

SEQUENCE:
1. Name of company
2. Reason for story
3. Historical information
4. Unusual features if any
5. Quotations by principals
6. Explanation of features of business
7. Anecdotes and unusual facts
8. Location

Workshop

FOR IMMEDIATE RELEASE

A workshop for aspiring fiction writers will be held four successive Mondays from 8 to 10 PM beginning July 9 at the Johnson City Community House.

Headed by Louise Watson Jones, managing editor of Fiction House Publishing Company, each session will include "hard" criticism of writings by participants. In addition to her editorial position, Ms. Jones is author of 13 children's books and many short stories for both the children's and adult market.

The workshop is sponsored by the Johnson City Writers' Club, comprised of individuals interested in professional writing who reside in and around Johnson City. President of the club is Howard McIntyre, 1414 Sterling Road, who commented that membership is open to any adult. Dues are $10 per year, which includes a monthly newsletter and regular meetings, held the third Tuesday of each month at the Community House.

Participation in the workshop, which will be limited to 20, is $25 for members of the Johnson City Writers' Club and $30 for nonmembers. Reservations may be placed by calling Mr. McIntyre at 555-9876.

#####

SEQUENCE:
1. Name of event
2. Dates, time of day, and location
3. Name and credentials of workshop leader
4. Identification and credentials of sponsoring organization
5. Cost
6. Method of participation

Example of Fact Sheet

FACT SHEET

GRAND OPENING—"JUST RAGS" FASHIONS

WHERE:	9595 Eighth Street, Maryville
WHEN:	Saturday, June 10, 1978, 9 AM to 6 PM
WHAT:	An orchid will be given to every visitor to the store. Prizes will be awarded every hour.

Fashion show at 1 PM, showing preview of fall styles. Show will be conducted and narrated by Louise Morgan, writer of the column "This Week in Fashion" in the Maryville *Times.*

Julia Madden, star of *Rocks in His Head* at the Blackstone Theatre, will be at the store from 3 to 4 PM. Ten pairs of free tickets to the show will be given to visitors.

WHO:	"Just Rags" is owned by Justine Ragland, who first opened the boutique at 909 Adams Avenue in 1973. Ms. Ragland is a noted local fashion authority who makes two buying trips to Europe each year.
ADDITIONAL INFORMATION:	The new store is more than twice the size of the original store on Adams Avenue. With more than 2,000 square feet, it will be one of the largest fashion shops in

Maryville, specializing in reproductions of the latest high-fashion styles from Paris and Rome. A special "Silk Rag Salon" will feature originals direct from such designers as Givenchy and Christian Dior. Another department, "The Rag Bag," will offer discontinued lines at a discount. The "Stones and Bones" counter will include costume jewelry made of semi-precious stones, ivory, and jade.

CONTACT:

Ms. Joanne Lindsay
Just Rags
9595 Eighth Street
Maryville, California 92233
(415) 555-8765

index

247